Macmillan Business Masters

Marketing Research

Macmillan Business Masters

Marketing Research

Chris West

© Chris West 1999

All rights reserved. No reproduction, copy or transmission of
this publication may be made without written permission.

No paragraph of this publication may be reproduced, copied or
transmitted save with written permission or in accordance with
the provisions of the Copyright, Designs and Patents Act 1988,
or under the terms of any licence permitting limited copying
issued by the Copyright Licensing Agency, 90 Tottenham Court
Road, London W1P 9HE.

Any person who does any unauthorised act in relation to this
publication may be liable to criminal prosecution and civil
claims for damages.

The author has asserted his right to be identified
as the author of this work in accordance with the
Copyright, Designs and Patents Act 1988.

First published 1999 by
MACMILLAN PRESS LTD
Houndmills, Basingstoke, Hampshire RG21 6XS
and London
Companies and representatives
throughout the world

ISBN 0–333–72178–0

A catalogue record for this book is available from the British Library.

This book is printed on paper suitable for recycling and made from
fully managed and sustained forest sources

10   9   8   7   6   5   4   3   2   1
08   07   06   05   04   03   02   01   00   99

Copy-edited and typeset by Povey–Edmondson
Tavistock and Rochdale, England

Printed and bound in Great Britain by
Antony Rowe Ltd, Chippenham, Wiltshire

To
Frances, Simon, Alex and Kelly
without whom none of this would have been necessary!

Contents

List of Boxes

Preface

There are two types of books on market researching. The first is written for students and serious research practitioners and is devoted largely to techniques. The second is written for research users and, while covering techniques, is devoted primarily to the applications for research and the methods by which research data can be acquired. This book falls into the latter category and its intended audience is the large group of junior, middle and senior marketing management who have regular or occasional requirements for information who may wish to carry out surveys themselves but who are more likely to commission surveys from research professionals. ('Market' Research is the colloquial term used within and outside the profession, though 'Marketing' Research is the more accurate description. Both are used more or less interchangeably in this book.)

Obtaining market information can be undertaken in a wide variety of ways. Some of these are highly formalised and some are completely informal. There is often an assumption that formal, structured and scientific approaches to collecting information provide the best results but, as any businessman will tell you, the most useful pieces of information can just as easily come from casual conversations with colleagues, from salespeople's reports or from contacts made at a trade show, none of which could be described as either 'formal' or 'scientific'.

This book is about market research but it uses a broader definition than the sample survey techniques described in most academic texts. It is written for all types of information user and meets the needs of those whose budgets may not stretch to large-scale surveys as well as those whose needs require the use of the most advanced research techniques.

The information business is undergoing radical change initiated by developments in electronics and communications. What was once a cottage industry dependent entirely on people – research executives, interviewers and statisticians – is rapidly being transformed into a factory business using machines to manufacture statistics: it is in the throes of the information industry's equivalent of the industrial revolution. The effects are largely beneficial for all information users. At the lower end of the scale the internet, intranets and the ever-widening range of databases are making it easier to access ready-made market information quickly and cost effectively. Even those with minimal research budgets can therefore compile a rough and ready portrait of their market. At the other end of the scale, those with more sophisticated research needs are being bombarded with new processes and the techniques designed to implement them. The research press continuously describes new data collection methods and new analysis tools which improve the efficiency of the research process, correct some of the problems endemic in the research process, add to the quality of the data and, in some cases, even reduce costs.

The wider availability and lower cost of information mean that there is less excuse for not using it. At one time research was considered so expensive that it was seen to be the preserve of the larger corporations. This is no longer the case, and whereas it was once possible for smaller organisations to assume that most of their competitors were equally ignorant about their markets, to do so now would be courting disaster. Today the company with the better mousetrap is much more likely to have analysed customer requirements, tested the concept, estimated potential demand, researched customer satisfaction with existing products and obtained intelligence on its competitors before it launched the product.

This book sets out to answer the most basic questions that marketing managers need to address when deciding whether to use research and how to go about obtaining market information. In summary these are:

- How do I **define** the information that is required for good marketing decision making?
- What internal and external **sources** of information can I consider using?
- What **research techniques** can be used?
- How do I define a **research project** that will meet my requirements?
- How can I work with **external research consultants**?
- How do I initiate and monitor a **research project**?
- How do I assess the **quality of the results** and integrate them into my market planning?

In the process of answering these questions the book covers research techniques in considerable detail, and therefore answers a further question, namely, how do I do research?

How to do research is a topic I have been attempting to address for the last 35 years – not an easy task in a field where the goalposts are continuously moving. I have come to it as one whose clients are primarily companies selling into industrial rather than consumer markets. This branch of the research business used to be called 'industrial market research' but there are some that have tried to re-christen it 'business-to-business' research. Arguments about semantics are rarely productive and I do not propose to engage in them here. Nor do I propose to invent a new title for the business which embraces all methods of collecting, analysing and interpreting market information. Market research serves well enough for that purpose, provided it is clear that sample survey techniques are not the only methods by which market data can be collected – a heretical thought to some in the business.

In learning my trade I am grateful to all of my current and former colleagues in the three market research companies in which I have worked in, run and, in two cases, been a founder Director – Industrial Market Research (IMR), Business Marketing Services (BMSL) and Marketing Intelligence Services (MIS). However, I owe my biggest debt of gratitude to Aubrey Wilson, the founder of IMR, who enticed me into the business and has been a mentor, colleague and friend ever since. Aubrey's own writings on market research were seminal works in their day and, given the changes that have taken place, have stood the test of time remarkably well. If I have an idiosyncratic and pragmatic view of the research business I blame Aubrey completely. He taught me long ago that 'arriving was infinitely better than travelling hopefully'. By this I mean that clients who commission research projects are primarily interested in obtaining a **timely and accurate solution** to their problem. How that solution is obtained is immaterial, as long as the findings are right, can be shown to be right, and are on time. For every client that is deeply interested in research techniques and the jargon that accompanies them, there are hundreds that are interested only in the final output and what it means. For them, the results of a few well-placed telephone calls and hurried calculations can be just as valuable as an extensive market survey. Any other failings in this book are entirely my own.

CHRIS WEST

1 Introduction

1.1 What is Market Research?

Market research is a term which can mean different things to different people. To most professional market researchers it means the use of a defined set of qualitative or quantitative research techniques to obtain data which describes and analyses markets or potential markets. To the layman it means 'surveys'. A word association test carried out on 'market research' will invariably produce responses such as 'clipboard', 'interviewer' or 'statistics' – classic ingredients of a sample survey. Another common response is 'waste of time', meaning 'a waste of my time on the street, in the home or at an airport when I am asked to provide information'. The relationship between research and surveys is a strong one but to the businessperson, market research encompasses any activity which provides him with the market information he or she needs. There is therefore a narrow definition, which covers quantitative and qualitative surveys, and a broad definition, which extends to all formal and informal methods of acquiring information.

1.2 The Origins and Growth of Market Research

The **systematic collection of information for planning** is as old as government, though it would be stretching a point to cite the censuses of Biblical times and the Domesday Book as the antecedents of modern market research. Some of the output of today's research business has much in common with the surveys carried out by nineteenth-century sociologists such as Edwin Chadwick (*Report on the Sanitary Conditions of the Labouring Population*, 1842), Charles Booth (*Life and Labour of the People of London*, 1889) and Seebohm Rowntree (*Poverty: A Study of Town Life*, 1901), but the commercial research business in fact originated in 1824, when the *Harrisburg Pennsylvanian* newspaper sent out reporters to conduct a 'straw poll' on presidential voting intentions among the citizens of Wilmington. Other US newspapers followed the lead in subsequent elections and opinion polling has remained a major contributor to the incomes of research agencies to this day.

Most of the early **market research** undertaken in the USA was related to advertising. The first attempt at formal market analysis took place in 1879, when N. W. Ayer & Son, the oldest US advertising agency, conducted a survey of US grain production by state and the circulation of relevant

1

journals in the farming community. This was used to develop an advertising campaign for a client that manufactured agricultural machinery. In the following years a number of studies into advertising-related topics were carried out marking the beginning of a long-standing relationship between advertising and market research. These included a survey in 1911 by R. O. Eastman of the Kellogg Company into magazine readership which used a mailed questionnaire. The results were used to plan advertising media schedules. To this day much of the research carried out is driven by the needs of advertisers, and advertising agencies are still major originators of research projects and users of research data.

Until the First World War most research activity was carried out either by individual researchers, university departments or by research staff operating within manufacturing companies. Collectively they developed and pioneered the sampling, data collection and analysis techniques that are still in use today. From this time on, the body of survey research literature began to develop.

The first years of the twentieth century saw sufficient growth in the demand for market research to justify the formation of dedicated research agencies. In most cases they were founded by academics or corporate market researchers who saw an opportunity for entrepreneurial activity. The first of these, Business Bourse, was formed in 1908 by J. George Frederick and he was followed by a number of others (including R. O. Eastman mentioned above) who had established their research reputations whilst working as employees. As a service business with low entry costs, market research has continued to attract professionals who would rather work for themselves than somebody else.

One of the most significant of the early arrivals was Arthur C. Nielsen who established the A. C. Nielsen company in 1923 and was responsible for the initiation of many of the major research services which account for a high proportion of research expenditure to this day, including retail audits and audience measurement. Art Nielsen was trained as an electrical engineer and his first research offerings were economic and engineering analyses to manufacturers of industrial products. After the depression in the 1920s he launched the Nielsen Drug Index followed by the Nielsen Food Index. Both of these were retail audits providing manufacturers with a tool by which they could track sales and their market shares. In 1936, Nielsen started a service to measure radio audiences using 'audiometers'; these recorded the stations to which a sample of radio sets were tuned. Radio research led on to the development of television ratings.

In the UK commercial market research activity based on survey techniques began later than in the USA, but the early days were similarly linked to advertising and media. Both J. Walter Thompson and the London Press Exchange initiated research projects in the 1920s and in 1922 the Publicity Club of London established the Bureau of Advertising Facts to collect data for the advertising industry; this organisation remained active until 1935. The first independent research company, the London Research and Information Bureau, was formed in 1923. Sales Research Services (which subsequently became part of Taylor Nelson) was formed in 1928 and this was followed by a number of companies that have dominated the business at various times since. Bedford Attwood, later the founder of Attwood Statistics, formed a research unit within J. Walter Thompson in 1931; the British Market Research Bureau (now part of WPP) was formed in 1933; the British Institute of Public Opinion (later to become Gallup) was formed by Dr Henry Durant in 1936; Mass Observation, later acquired by Burke, was also formed in 1936. Nielsen established their UK subsidiary in 1939 at the instigation of Unilever, who later became a major player in the business themselves when they formed and then span off Research International.

The rate of research company formation was supported by continued growth in the demand for research services during the 1930s. The advertising agencies continued to be major drivers of growth. Advertising was itself a growing business and as advertising costs rose there was an increasing need for market and media research to ensure that the right messages were directed at the right target audiences. At the same time increasing competition and increasing risk attached to the launch of new products. Furthermore, customers started to become more sophisticated in terms of their requirements and the trial and error approach to product development and selling became less acceptable. Larger companies responded by establishing sales and marketing departments who needed information to support their strategies. Government also played a role in promoting the use of market research: the Ministry of Food initiated the National Food Survey in 1940 and the Government Social Survey was established in 1941.

In the period following the end of the Second World War the research industry has refined its techniques and extended the coverage of its surveys. This was accompanied by a major increase in the number of companies offering research services and the emergence of sizeable research groups. Nevertheless, the entrepreneurial nature of research business, noted in its earliest days, has remained a distinctive characteristic. Research companies, even the largest, have come and gone or been absorbed by others. The mainstay of the business has continued to be small research companies which rely on the talents of a limited number of researchers.

1.3 The Research Business Today

Over the last 20 years the agency side of the market research business has not only grown but also fragmented into an ever-increasing number of specialisations. The business has been characterised by the growth of a limited number of very large research companies and a proliferation of small companies. The number of large research companies that have remained independent has been reduced drastically as the big names such as Nielsen, Research International, BMRB Survey Research Group and Milward Brown have been absorbed by information and marketing services groups. At the bottom of the pile the formation of new research companies continues apace. Some of these struggle out of the mire and manage to develop into medium-sized companies. At this point they are often acquired or merge to maintain the pace of development of the larger companies and ensure the survival of the organisation once the founder decides to hang up his clipboard.

The fecundity of the research business and the process of fragmentation are interlinked and driven partly by ego and partly by technology. Research companies are relatively easy to establish and there has never been a shortage of researchers who prize their independence sufficiently to take the risk of forming their own operation. Technology has provided opportunities for individual researchers to exploit niches within the research business. Whereas researchers were once generalists using a range of techniques to obtain information designed to solve a variety of business problems, increasing numbers now focus on the use of a specialist technique or a particular type of marketing problem or a specialist market segment. The earliest divisions of research activity were between the major applications for research. Opinion polling, advertising and media research, social research and market analysis provided the earliest threads within the fabric of research activity. A split between quantitative research and qualitative research emerged in response to the activities of motivational researchers. There was then a group that specialised in the analysis of industrial as opposed to consumer markets. Next came the continuous researchers, who regularly monitored activity in markets and were separated from the ad hoc businesses which solved problems as they came along. Certain markets, some of them requiring specialist techniques or industry knowledge, attracted dedicated researchers. Thus medical, agricultural, children, chemical, automotive and information technology became recognised research specialisations.

Published research, databases and multi-client studies are another significant post-war development within the research business. Research users generally want their data quick and cheap, requirements which researchers producing customised surveys find hard to fulfil. However, the supply of instant information has expanded as a variety of publishers have entered the market with large portfolios of reports. Topic selection has to take into account the sales potential for the information and therefore avoids the esoteric in favour of the popular, but the number of studies which are available is nevertheless sufficiently broad to meet a diverse range of requirements.

A range of services designed to support research activity also evolved into separate activities – field research, data prep and processing and organisations specialising in analysis techniques have all developed as important facilitators of research activity. The range of services that are available is such that 'virtual research companies' are easy to establish. Individuals with the client handling and analytical skills have little difficulty in running substantial research programmes from their homes by buying in all of the individual research services they require.

1.4 Global Research

As marketing has globalised so have the requirements for research data that is consistent between countries. This has provided a opportunity for the research business to globalise itself. Many of the larger research groups now operate on a multinational basis and smaller companies have established alliances which enable them to offer clients a multi-country research service.

1.5 In-house Researchers

The research business has always comprised researchers who are employed by companies that use research results (in-house researchers) and external, independent research suppliers. Internal research departments were once large and self-sufficient. Although relatively few, and mainly large, companies had them, they were major contributors to the development of market research. In one notable case, the internal research department for Unilever was spun off as a separate company and subsequently became a major force in the industry – Research International.

The heyday of the large internal market research department was in the 1960s and early 1970s but during the subsequent recessions axing the market research department was one of the easiest cost-saving decisions to take. The demise of the in-house research department aided the growth of the research agencies who were relied on increasingly to provide data.

Where they still exist, in-house researchers may still carry out research themselves but are more commonly the link between internal research users and external agencies who carry out projects on their behalf. The in-house researcher uses his skills to define the research approach that will solve his client's problem, commissions the agency, monitors the progress of the study, adds value to the final results by interpreting them in the light of his company knowledge, and presents the results to the decision makers.

1.6 What Does the Research Business Offer?

The research business offers its clients data on any aspect of a market that can be studied by ethical research techniques. This means that there is information which researchers cannot and should not set out to obtain because to do so would place them in breach of the various codes of practice of the research business. However, this still leaves a vast range of topics which can be studied and which meet most of the requirements of research users.

The canvas covered by this book is deliberately wider than the conventions of survey research covered in most academic texts. The techniques used in survey research can be applied in differing intensities and in different ways to produce results of varying levels of accuracy, depth, scope and detail. The main breakthrough in the development of the research business was the discovery of the statistical theory which showed that data collected from relatively small but representative samples of any given market could accurately describe the market as a whole. Up to that point it was thought that only a census could provide an accurate picture. The growth of the research business has been based largely on **sample surveys**. However, sample surveys tend to be costly and beyond the reach of smaller companies or unnecessarily expensive for many of the problems the data is required to solve.

The research industry has responded by providing **business intelligence services**. These use standard research techniques but do not apply them to representative samples of respondents. It is evident that a fact is no less a fact even if it is derived from a single respondent, provided it can be shown to be accurate. Business intelligence relies on multiple research approaches, highly targeted interviewing, and checking procedures in order to develop the types of data generated by sample surveys, at equivalent levels of accuracy, more quickly and at lower cost. If this sounds the answer to marketing manager's prayer it sometimes is, but not always. Business intelligence relies on the assumption that someone out there knows the answers, and while this is often the case it is not always so. Market sizing, market shares and the structure of distribution can commonly be obtained using a business intelligence approach, but it is much less useful for qualitative information of all types.

Marketing and market research has evolved to the point where manufacturers and suppliers of services who are serious about meeting customer requirements all have access to the same data. This has resulted in a situation in which the offers from competing companies have become less and less differentiated. At the same time, slow growth in demand means that suppliers have to seek an increase in market share in order to reach ambitious sales targets. Even if they are not seeking to grow faster than the market, companies may still need to defend themselves against others that are. Both situations require a competitive strategy which in turn needs to be based on **competitive intelligence**. The provision of information about the activities and performance of specific suppliers has been an objective of survey research and business intelligence for many years. For example, retail audits and customer satisfaction surveys can both provide comparative information on competitors. However, the intelligence needs for a competitive strategy can go a lot further, such as predicting the possible future actions of competitors in order anticipate challenges that could arise. To meet these needs competitive intelligence has emerged as a separate discipline with its own code of ethics and techniques adapted to the special situations in which the research takes place.

1.7 **Informal Market Research**

The contribution of informal research must be acknowledged, largely because it is widely practised. For many companies informal discussions with distributors, key customers and competitors is the *only* type of research that is carried out and, although it is important to point out that it is fraught with problems, it is indisputably research into the market and the professional researcher would have to have a particular affinity for sticking his or her head into the sand to insist that informal approaches cannot yield valuable information. Unfortunately, the professional researcher is right to be sceptical. All information obtained by informal methods is open to challenge. Without proper controls over the way the research is done, the information could easily be inaccurate or biased, or both, the results accepted only because they confirm existing opinions and prejudices and acceptable because the data collection process incurs minimal cost.

The most common informal method of collecting information is via the salesforce. Salespeople have a unique opportunity to obtain information during their calls on customers and distributors. Although data collection by the salesforce can be formalised, this rarely happens. Salespeople's reports which contain information on specific customers and prospects, and may be laced with industry gossip, are simply not designed to provide a systematic review of the market as a whole. There is also a deeper problem which arises from the inadequacies of salespeople as information collectors. The characteristics of good salespeople are diametrically opposed to those of good researchers. Whereas the researcher needs to be neutral and a good listener the salesman needs to be completely biased in favour of his product and an ardent advocate of his company. Furthermore, those who provide information to salespeople know precisely what is going to happen to it and it is not unknown for inaccurate information to be planted by customers for some tactical or strategic purpose. The area in which this is likely to be most pronounced is that of pricing. In a negotiating situation individual and business customers will commonly state that competitors have offered them lower prices, bigger discounts or more favourable payment terms in order to exert price pressure on suppliers. This is not to say that salespeople are incapable of obtaining reliable information, only that what they do obtain needs to be treated with caution and checked carefully before it is accepted.

1.8 Market Research People

As with any service the quality of a research organisation, be it a specialist research company or an internal department, is only as good as the people within it. Most organisations have systems to ensure that research is carried out correctly but the final product is still largely dependent on the people who carry out the research. Most research organisations have a similar structure (see Box 1.1).

The Directors, be they full or Associate Directors, are the staff with the most experience. They are the primary interface between the research company (or department) and the client. In small research companies they maintain a watching brief over projects and are involved in the key stages of the project, particularly the final interpretation of the findings. Directors may also be responsible for selling their companies' services but in the larger research companies there are generally sales teams (sometimes called Client Service Executives) who carry out the sales function. Project Managers, as their name implies, manage the projects and provide day-to-day guidance and control to research executives. Research executives of varying levels of seniority carry out the research work either themselves or with the assistance of Research Assistants and the field department.

The field department is the engine room of most research companies. Fieldworkers collect the primary data inputs from respondents and the entire research process depends on the effectiveness with which they carry out their role. Most fieldworkers are freelancers and are commonly paid piece rates rather than a salary. They are distributed throughout the country and work in their own localities. This creates a requirement for strong supervision in terms of both field managers and field supervisors and supervision systems.

The technical specialists include specification writers, statisticians and data processing experts. The latter are gradually being displaced by user-

---

Box 1.1 Structure of research organisations

- Directors
- Salespeople
- Project managers
- Senior research executives
- Research executives
- Research assistants
- Field management
- Fieldworkers
- Technical specialists
- Administrative staff
- Freelance research consultants.

friendly software which enables executives to carry out analyses formerly the province of the experts, but for the more sophisticated research and for large-scale projects systems people are still required.

Research organisations of all types generate large amounts of paper. Although this is being reduced as more wide-scale use is made of electronic data collection techniques, a good administrative system is required to ensure that the organisation runs smoothly and that vital documents are correctly stored and can be retrieved.

Freelance research consultants are a mixed band of ex-employees of research companies or marketing departments. They work on their own account for clients but also take projects on sub-contract from research companies in an overload situation. They can bring a wealth of experience to projects which is sometimes difficult to achieve with the younger employees.

A high proportion of the employees in the research business are graduates at the beginning of their careers. Research is an excellent training ground for senior marketers and is used as such by those who see it as a stepping stone. The industry cannot offer a full career opportunity for all those that enter the business and most research companies see no harm in having their alumni located in senior marketing positions in industry.

1.9 Who Uses Market Research?

Any organisation can use market research and the client base for the industry is certainly extremely broad. However, given its main activity – the analysis of markets – the research business is remarkably uninformed about the environment it operates within. This is something to do with the 'cobbler's children syndrome'[1] but also reflects the fact that research expenditure has grown healthily, the marketing of research agencies is relatively primitive and competition between research providers tends to be considerably less intense than that experienced in the markets for products. Research shares these characteristics with most other professions, most of whom have had to be dragged screaming into the marketing age and still refuse to raise their marketing game.

Nevertheless, one survey[2] carried out in the UK showed what most researchers knew intuitively, namely that the overall commitment to research is low and that use of research is extremely patchy. Large companies are far more likely to use market research than small companies. 60 per cent of companies with sales under £2.5 million had no research budget but this figure falls substantially as the size of company increases, reaching 15 per cent for companies with sales in excess of £20 million. Fast moving consumer goods (FMCG) suppliers are twice as likely to use market research as all other types of company, which explains why the consumer market research business is significantly larger than its industrial counterpart. The research also demonstrated that companies which use market research are more likely to make above-average profits and less likely to incur losses. No causal relationship could be demonstrated – i.e. there was no way of proving that the research input brought about better performance, but there was a clear inference that research use is at least a consequence of a management style which produces above-average profits.

The reasons why companies do not use research are usually put down to the fact that they feel they already know all that there is to know about their markets and that the cost cannot be justified. However, it has also been shown that some companies have a research culture whilst others do not. In the case of the former they are significantly more likely to pre- and post-test their marketing proposals using research as a key input.

1.10 **The Importance of Research**

Research has long passed the point at which it provides 'nice to know' information of the sort which makes interesting editorial copy. It not only drives a high proportion of new product development but also forms an integral part of the marketing planning process of most major corporations and can also provide the basis for important financial transactions (Box 1.2).

With stakes this high, the research must be accurate and acceptable to all the parties concerned.

Box 1.2 The importance of research

- The **advertising revenues** of television channels depend on the sizes of audiences measured by television audience research programmes
- The **performance bonuses** of many company executives depend on the achievement of customer satisfaction targets, which are recorded by means of customer satisfaction surveys
- Since deregulation, parts of the **revenue generated by the London bus system** (some £350 million which is not collected by operators on the buses themselves) is apportioned between bus operators on the basis of a survey of passengers.

Notes

1. 'The cobbler's children being the least well shod'.
2. Graham Hooley and Chris West, 'The Untapped Markets for Marketing Research', *Journal of the Market Research Society* (1984), pp. 335–52.

2 Knowledge-based Marketing

Knowledge is the fuel which powers all decision making. Other things being equal, good knowledge will result in good decisions and poor or inadequate knowledge will lead to bad decisions. Market research is the process by which companies acquire knowledge of the market places in which they operate, or would like to operate, in order to provide a firm foundation for marketing decisions.

2.1 Marketing Research and the Marketing Knowledge Base

Organisations use many types of resources to function, of which one of the most valuable, but often the least understood, is their **knowledge base** (Box 2.1). Without knowledge, management is unable to take informed decisions and the quality of knowledge may be all that distinguishes a successful from an unsuccessful organisation. Knowledge, like skills, resides primarily in employees but can also be collected in databases, reports, patents, plans, budgets, memoranda and a variety of other documents. The knowledge base covers all aspects of the organisation's activities – products, technology, human resources, finance, sales and marketing – and is a wasting asset requiring constant updating, improvement and extension to keep pace with changes in the operating environment.

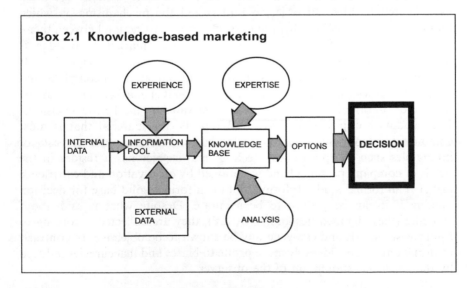

Box 2.1 Knowledge-based marketing

Nowhere is the need for detailed, accurate and up-to-date knowledge more evident than in the marketing function. Markets have two characteristics which distinguish them from the other environments in which companies operate (see Box 2.2).

Box 2.2 The modern marketing environment

- Markets are invariably **dynamic** and are tending to become more so in response to the increasing pace of technical development, competitive pressure and a continual uplift in customers' expectations.
- Change is caused by a wide diversity of factors, most of which are **beyond the control of any single supplier**.

Marketing therefore operates in an inherently unstable environment and it is all too easy for companies to lose touch with conditions in the markets they service. Furthermore, in the quest for growth, or even to defend existing market positions, the problem tends to be exacerbated by the fact that companies continually need to do something new. They develop new strategies, launch new products, target new markets and initiate new service packages, all of which push them into increasingly unfamiliar marketing territory.

The antidote to these conditions is a marketing knowledge base which is updated and extended in line with the development of the business.

2.2 Data, Information and Knowledge

The words 'data', 'information', 'knowledge' and even 'wisdom' are often used interchangeably. In order to understand the mechanisms by which knowledge is acquired, it is helpful to draw a clear distinction between them.

Market data is the raw material from which market knowledge is ultimately derived – the raw ingredients used to make a recipe dish. It comprises sets of facts, sometimes complete and sometimes incomplete, and sometimes of varying degrees of accuracy about a market. Data can be formal or informal, and both can be relevant to marketing decisions. Formal data consists of statistics and reports, the material that is most commonly entered into marketing databases. Informal data consists of intangibles such as appearances, feelings and suspicions. It resides in the heads of company personnel and is obtained by observation and experience rather than formal study. Informal data can form a solid base for decision making if it can be proven to be accurate. Despite what is said about statistics ('lies, damned lies and statistics'), they are collected according to rigorous standards and can generally be shown to be objective. In contrast, informal data is considerably more prone to biases and inaccuracies induced by the particular standpoint of the observer.

A high proportion of marketing decisions, particularly in smaller organisations, are driven by informal rather than formal data. The informal generally takes over when there is a lack of formal data; this can arise when formal data it is too costly to acquire or there is insufficient time or when management feels that its informal data are sufficient for the task.

Most companies have an array of data on the markets in which they operate. Whether they have converted their data into **information** is less certain. Information is obtained by digesting data and converting it into patterns. During the process discrete items of data are assembled together, contradictory items of information are reconciled, missing information is interpolated, inaccurate data is identified and discarded and the overall picture of the marketplace that emerges is deepened.

Knowledge results from the interpretation of information in order to understand what it means and how it can be acted upon. The interpretative process uses analysis and expertise to show not only how markets operate but also the threats and opportunities which exist and likely consequences of actions by suppliers.

Wisdom is the result of long periods of assimilating knowledge. A wise person (or organisation) is one who knows from experience what is right. They rely less on new inputs of knowledge to reach a conclusion, though if the basis of wisdom is not periodically re-calibrated by inputting current conditions it, too, can become out of date.

2.3 The Contribution of Market Research to the Knowledge Base

Many companies rely exclusively on informal knowledge bases derived from their own internal experience and expertise. This can be adequate, particularly when covering specialised markets in which companies have operated for some time. Nevertheless, there is always a risk that knowledge derived exclusively from experience will be incomplete, outdated or inaccurate. This risk increases if markets become subject to rapid change or if companies consider businesses which are removed from their core activities and where their direct experience is limited.

The key ingredient to an adequate knowledge base is **market data and market information derived from sources active within the marketplace itself**, notably customers, competitors, distributors, regulators and advisors (Box 2.3). To be of maximum value market data needs to be collected independently, using methods which are separated from the routine internal contacts with the marketplace – such as sales and service activities. Data which flows through internal channels has its place and must be encouraged and harvested, but it is unlikely to be sufficiently detailed or complete to meet the needs of market planners. It may also be subject to error and bias which renders it useless.

Box 2.3 Marketing research

Marketing research is the marketing service which:

- collects market data by means of a set of **formal techniques**
- analyses and interprets data to create **market information**
- presents the results to marketing management who will use it to create a knowledge base which will act as a foundation for **marketing decision taking**.

2.4 Users of Marketing Research

The mainstream users of marketing research are all types of commercial organisations who require market knowledge to assist them improve the quality of their marketing decisions. Suppliers of raw materials, manufacturers, distributors, suppliers of professional and other services are the main initiators of marketing research surveys. They are sometimes joined by organisations and institutions who participate indirectly in the marketing process or who need to observe what is happening in markets for purposes other than marketing management. Trade associations commission research on behalf of their members; government agencies with a marketing mandate, such as tourist boards, commission research to obtain the data they require to direct their promotional activity; television channels, newspapers, the trade press and exhibition organisers commission research to demonstrate the effectiveness of their media as promotional vehicles and, in some instances, to obtain editorial copy.

Some confusion arises from the fact that the survey techniques used by marketing researchers are also used to obtain information which has no marketing application, unless a very liberal definition of 'marketing' is adopted. Opinion polls, which provide a substantial income stream to research companies, are arguably part of the information input required by political parties to market themselves to the electorate and research into attitudes towards government policy forms a basis for government marketing strategies; but investigations into housing conditions, community health or wage and salary levels is in reality social and political research which has little, if any, connection with marketing.

3   Marketing Information and Knowledge Management

The fact that information is **collected** does not automatically mean that it is **used**. Although those responsible for defining information requirements and for commissioning research surveys obviously have an interest in applying the results, there is no certainty that the remainder of the organisation will be able to contribute to the information collection process or have access to the results unless a formal marketing information system is in place. Indeed, following the principle that 'knowledge is power', there is every chance that those holding information will keep it to themselves and key decision makers may be left unaware that market information exists within the organisation.

3.1 Knowledge Management

The problem of integrating knowledge into the decision making processes of a company is not unique to marketing. Most other corporate functions use information which needs to be collected, processed, interpreted and distributed and there can be considerable overlap in the information needs of departments. For example, current sales information is relevant not only to the marketing department but also to finance, production and planning. Knowledge management is a new discipline which encompasses the **total information needs** of a company which are obtained from internal and external sources. It feeds into all business processes and integrates hard data with 'soft' assets of an organisation, namely the creative contributions that can be made by staff.

A key difference from traditional information systems is that knowledge management acknowledges the importance not only of **explicit knowledge** – that which is written down and incorporated in inventories – but also **tacit knowledge** – the understanding that individual staff members carry around in their heads or in local records to enable them to carry out their tasks. Within the marketing function, for example, salespeople represent a major repository of information which is rarely acknowledged let alone brought together. Even though it may be subject to all sorts of distortions and biases, it can, if brought together, provide considerable insight into the status and development of a market. The focus of the picture of the market that is provided may be considerably sharpened when data from all salespeople is compared and rationalised.

The system improves efficiency by increasing the availability and use of the information assets that the company has acquired by:

- tapping the **data collection and creative resources** of all relevant staff in the organisation
- minimising the chances of the same tasks being **repeated** in separate parts of the organisation
- making a **consensus interpretation** available to all
- maintaining the **currency of the information**.

Knowledge management systems are usually associated with powerful computer hardware and software, such as Lotus Notes, which is capable of handling large amounts of data. The hardware and software are indeed a valuable component, especially in large organisations, but are not essential to the process. The primary task is to gain acceptance that knowledge is required throughout the organisation and that it can be created and distributed if all of the relevant staff have access to raw data and can work on it for their own purposes and for the common benefit of the system. This can be achieved manually without the burden of designing an automated system. Indeed, it is advisable to establish a manual system and prove that it works and is accepted before major investments in hardware and software are made.

Nevertheless a growing number of custom-designed knowledge management systems are being developed and made available to organisations that embrace the concept. Some typical systems are described below and have been selected to show how knowledge management differs fundamentally from more traditional methods of sharing information within organisations.[1]

Knowledgex (http://www.knowledgeex.com)

A software application for acquiring, discovering, publishing and distributing knowledge across an organisation. It aims to tap into employees' knowledge about a market, to share this information with people who need to know and to develop a knowledge base with a simple-to-use visual interface.

6DOS (http://www.6dos.com)

This system offers connecting, tracking and rewarding facilities. The connecting facility provides a question and answer system to help reach those individuals within an organisation who will know the answers to questions. The tracking function follows through the flow of information of questions and answers to create an archive for re-use. The rewarding function encourages people in the organisation to participate by providing incentives.

Wisewire (http://www.wisewire.com)

Wisewire is held on an organisation's web site or intranet. It feeds in real-time information or delivers personalised profiles to interested parties. The content comprises online sources, premium sources, newsgroups, mailing lists and the organisation's own proprietary information. The most relevant information can be archived to provide a searchable resource.

Intraspect (http://www.intraspect.com)

Intraspect enables the collection, organisation and re-use of information via a single interface. The contents of the organisation's memory are indexed to enable filtered and focused searching. The search results show the contexts of the returned documents so the user can easily see what parts of the organisation are relevant. Comments can be attached to documents and discussion groups set up through the interface or by e-mail.

Intranets

Intranets, the internal equivalent of the internet (see Chapter 12), are rapidly gaining acceptance as a vehicle for collecting and sharing information within organisations. However, the intranet is a passive participant in the knowledge management process. It connects information gatherers with information users but does not in itself overcome the cultural problems which act as a barrier to information exchange. Nor can it filter or manipulate information unless the types of software packages described above are installed on it.

3.2 Marketing Information Systems

A traditional marketing information system (MIS) is a mechanism by which market information is collected, verified, analysed, stored and continuously fed out to those responsible for making marketing decisions. Although marketing information systems existed long before knowledge management hit the desks of unwary management, they can clearly be an important component of knowledge management systems and will benefit from their functional capabilities – particularly their ability to incorporate automatic data feeds from the internet and other external sources (see Chapters 6 and 12).

MIS can be designed to ensure that market analysis is undertaken regularly, that full use is made of internal and external information sources and that the information collected and stored is tailored to the specific needs of the company. Without a system, market analysis tends to be spasmodic, undertaken only when the problem is sufficiently serious and when sufficient time is available to collect data. This may result in important decisions being taken without the necessary information being made available to support them.

The need for an marketing information system becomes more acute as companies expand, the marketing staff expands and the number of major decisions increases. However, a marketing information system represents a major investment of time and resources and not all companies are likely to benefit to the same extent from a formal system. Small companies, those operating in static, undynamic markets, or companies active in highly concentrated businesses where the number of customers and competitors are few would find it hard to justify a major investment in a marketing information system. Indeed many such organisations are well served by a informal system which either collects information when it is required or holds a small manual database of relevant information.

Functions of a marketing information system

To be fully effective a marketing information system must be something more than a passive store of information. It also needs to be dynamic in the sense that it stimulates the flow of information to users and triggers the actions required to fill information gaps and ensures that the information available from the system is continuously updated to meet the changing needs of the organisation. This suggests a system which is an important component of the working environment of the marketing department and which is used continuously (Box 3.1).

By bringing together all of the information that a company collects from internal and external sources and by means of secondary and primary research, an effective marketing information system can not only improve information utilisation but can also save money. Regardless of the purpose for which the information was collected, it can often be recycled for other applications. Furthermore, large organisations can duplicate information collection costs as different departments specify the same information needs and either commission their own surveys or purchase the same published reports.

Information held in a marketing information system

To be useful, and to encourage staff to use it, a marketing information system must contain most (if not all) of the information which marketing managers require on a regular basis. This includes the formal and informal information referred to in Chapter 2.

While managers will accept that exceptional or unusual information needs, such as those related to a new product development, are not catered for by the system and therefore have to be resourced separately, they will

---

Box 3.1 The marketing information system

The key functions of an marketing information system are:

- to act as a **repository** for all information that is relevant to the company's marketing activities; this includes:
  - data generated internally from the company's own records
  - data collected regularly from key secondary sources
  - continuous and/or ad hoc survey data that has been purchased or commissioned from external sources
  - anecdotal information on customers, distributors and competitors collected by the salesforce and others having regular external contacts
- to ensure that the information which is used continuously is always **up to date**
- to sift and interpret incoming information, determine its accuracy and **grade its importance** to the company's current and future operations
- to identify **information gaps** either by matching information needs with information available on the system or by processing information requests from line managers
- to distribute data which has been acquired and alert management of significant **developments, threats and opportunities**.

---

soon run out of patience with a system which fails to answer routine questions (Box 3.2).

A system can also contain a facility for staff to enter information and interpretations of their own ('tacit' information), to make comments on data or trends for others in the company to consider and to request additional information. Security systems need to be in place to prevent information being overwritten or lost – and, more importantly, to prevent unauthorised access.

A marketing information system is unlikely to contain all of the information that a marketing department will ever require. Cost will be the main factor limiting that which is carried on a regular basis, but utilisation levels will also be an important consideration. It clearly makes sense for a system to carry data which is required on a regular basis but information that is obtained for a one-off application or is used only occasionally is rarely worth entering. Special studies carried out for specific purposes, such as assisting in the development of a new product, are best left off the system unless they contain environmental and market data which can be recycled for other applications.

Whilst there is no physical limit, other than storage space, to what is placed on an marketing information system, the system must be easy to navigate and users must be able to locate and retrieve the information they require quickly. Large systems need not be cumbersome but they must be well designed to make them user-friendly. Some of the standard software

---

Box 3.2 'Routine information'

The definition of what constitutes routine information will vary from company to company, as will become evident in later chapters, but it is likely to include:

- **Company data**, showing sales by product category, customer category, distribution channel and price level, margins, inventory levels, promotional expenditure and awareness levels
- **Market information** which enables the company to monitor its performance; this would include total demand volumes, demand by product type and market segment, flows through the alternative channels of distribution and price movements.
- **Information on competitors**, covering products, market share movements, prices, key accounts, promotional activities, staff changes and new developments
- **Computed information**, such as overall market shares and share by market segment and distribution channel
- **Forecasts** of sales and market structure
- **Environmental information** which affects market performance and strategy, regulatory information such as standards and government regulations
- **Qualitative information** covering customer use and attitude data and purchasing practices
- **News and gossip** culled from sales reports, news items and external intelligence sources

---

packages which have been developed to handle large-scale information systems are notoriously difficult to operate and may require considerable modification to make them acceptable.

Feeding the marketing information system

Like all databases, a marketing information system requires constant **management and updating**. In dynamic markets updating can be a daily task, in others the requirement may be less frequent. Data inputs, as we have shown, can come from a wide variety of sources within and outside the company and the management of the marketing information system, and control over what is placed on it, needs to be the responsibility of one person (or team of people). The primary management task is to ensure that what is placed on the marketing information system is relevant to the company's business, accurate and timely. Without proper stewardship the database will either atrophy and fall into disuse or will become so overloaded with irrelevant data, fed in by enthusiastic but uninformed staff, that it will become impossible to use efficiently. Anyone who doubts this need look only at the internet.

The management of the marketing information system should properly be the responsibility of a marketing information or business intelligence manager. In smaller companies where such functions do not exist, responsibility can reside with business development or marketing management. Where the upkeep of the marketing information system is a part-time responsibility it must be recognised that the process will be sporadic rather than continuous. This is not necessarily a problem. Updates will generally be organised when there is a need to use the data and whilst something may be lost in terms of detail and a time penalty will be incurred whilst the updating tales place, this may be a far more cost-efficient approach for companies where the runes do not require constant consultation in order to maintain an effective marketing programme.

Although the most common feed into the marketing information system is manual, increasing use is being made of automatic feeds from internal and external sources, thereby reducing the workloads on those responsible for administering the system. Automatic feeds can include data from other in-house financial and sales records and data feeds from external providers, such as those offering syndicated market research data, audience viewing statistics, environmental data or information culled from news media.

Format of the marketing information system

The use of the word system implies that all marketing information systems are fully electronic. This is far from being the case. Whilst the larger and more advanced systems are electronic, and are likely to be fully integrated into knowledge management systems as they are established, there are still large amounts of data which are held manually. A composite system in a large organisation will consist of written records (books, journals, reports, etc.), data held on data disks and CD ROMs and records held on computer files. The computer files may be accessed by the organisation either on local or wide area networks or via an intranet system. Small companies may rely entirely on written records (see Box 3.3).

The transition from manual to electronic systems can be painful if an attempt is made to convert all manually held records into an electronic format without careful planning. This should consider not only the volume of data to be handled and how it is to be organised but also how it is to be accessed and all of the applications it is to be used for. Manual systems tend to be self-regulating in that they place physical constraints on the amount of data that it collected and accessed. By relaxing these constraints, electronic systems create a risk of data overload which can paralyse decision making just as effectively as any lack of data. As always, time invested in the planning process will pay considerable dividends and it is often advisable to run manual and electronic systems side by side before converting to an entirely electronic approach.

Box 3.3 A composite MIS

Informal	Filing systems	Libraries	Electronic databases
Voice exchanges	Memos	Books	Company records
	Reports	Journals	Statistics
	Press clippings	Reports	Reports
		Statistical bulletins	Data feeds
		Disks	Analysis

Access to the marketing information system

A marketing information system needs to be accessed by senior marketing management, market planners, all line marketing staff including brand and product managers and sales staff and specialists such as advertising, PR and sales promotion staff. The needs of each individual will be different and in order to maintain high levels of security it is common for each staff member's access to be restricted to those parts of the database that he or she needs to fulfil their job function, and no more. Unlimited access to junior personnel poses severe security risks which are best avoided by removing temptation.

Note

1   The description of knowledge management systems has been obtained from EMG Ltd (http://www.emgltd.com), an organisation which specialises in knowledge management and in the provision of data. They produce a free newsletter on knowledge management which is available by e-mailing ted_howard-jones@emgltd.com.

4 Defining Marketing Information Needs

It may seem obvious but no market research project can commence unless there is a clear specification of the information that is required. The first – and often the most important – steps in a research exercise must therefore be devoted to assessing what information, or what mix of information, will help solve the marketing problems that are being considered.

4.1 Defining the Marketing Problem

All research commences with a problem. If there is no problem there is no need for research. Problems can arise anywhere within the marketing organisation and can be related to any part of the marketing process. Occasionally they may also arise outside the marketing organisation, such as those which relate to diversification or acquisition. The business development function can be as equally important a user of market research as the marketing department.

Research data can be required continuously or to solve periodic problems as and when they arise. Continuous data is used to monitor progress and, once agreed, becomes a regular and integral part of the marketing programme. Periodic problems arise out of:

- change within the marketplace
- a failure of actual performance to meet performance expectations
- a requirement to take new product or marketing initiatives.

Large marketing organisations, particularly those with major new product development programmes, can generate a constant stream of research problems. Companies operating in highly volatile and competitive markets can also face frequent marketing problems which require a knowledge-based solution.

Although the existence of a problem is a prerequisite for research, not all problems require market data in order to develop a solution, and if data is required it does not necessarily have to come from external sources.

Before specifying a research requirement it is essential to define the problem in terms which will show the required content, coverage, timing and scale of the research exercise. The problem is likely to originate in a either a

---

Box 4.1 Summary of marketing tasks

New product development
New product launches
Expansion of production capacity
Re-launches of existing products
Segmentation strategies
Distribution/marketing channel strategies
Sales strategies
Service strategies
Pricing strategies
Brand development
Packaging design
Advertising and promotional programme development
Awareness and image campaigns
Competitive strategies
Export marketing strategies
Responding to change in the market environment

---

strategic or **tactical situation** which the company is facing. Box 4.1 lists those tasks which most commonly create a need for information from the marketplace.

Although different situations require different mixes of information, a surprising number of marketing problems can be converted to a relatively short list of key marketing questions (Box 4.2).

There are a host of more esoteric problems which market research can solve but it tends to concentrate on fundamental analyses of the practices, requirements and attitudes of customers, distributors, specifiers and competitive suppliers that are active within a market in order to determine what should (or should not) be done to be successful.

Box 4.2 Key marketing questions

The most important of these are:

● **What** should I sell?
● **Who** should I sell it to?
● **How much** of it can I expect to sell?
● **What do I have** to do to sell it?
● **What territories** should I sell it in?
● **What prices** can I achieve?
● How am I **performing in my current markets**?
● What do I need to do to **beat the competition**?

Problem definition also needs to cover:

- The **geographical scope** of the exercise – what territories or which countries should be covered?
- The potential **financial or other rewards** that can be expected by solving the problem.
- The **amount of time** that is available to solve the problem.

Collectively these will determine the scale of the research exercise that is needed – and, therefore, its likely cost. There is no point in specifying a major research exercise unless the company is likely to make a gain which is commensurate with the cost.

4.2 Specification of Information Required

Defining the problem is an essential step to specifying the information which will solve it (Box 4.3).

Even within this relatively simple framework, research can help solve a wide diversity of marketing problems and the following paragraphs outline only the most common research applications.

Box 4.3 Market information

The main types of market information that can be obtained are:

- **Market measurements** – the sizes of markets, their structures and the trends that can be observed.
- **Customer research** – most importantly, their practices, intentions, attitudes, expectations, preferences, levels of satisfaction, purchasing procedures and exposure to communications media.
- **Channel research** – the effectiveness of alternative distribution channels and the requirements of distributors.
- **Competitive intelligence**.

Market measurement

A primary requirement for business planners is to set **achievable sales targets** and to show how these can be achieved. The quantitative element of a basic marketing plan for a product or service will show the planned sales progression (in volume or value), the customer groups that are to be targeted and the distribution channels that are to be used. To do this it is essential to know the total volume of sales that the market is absorbing (or is capable of absorbing) and the structure of the market. Sales data need to be broken down by product type or product category and the structural data need to show the channels through which products are distributed and the relationship between channels and customer groups. Sales targeting also requires detailed information on the **customer base** – who the purchasers of the product or service are, how large each purchasing group is and what relationships exist between the products purchased and the types of purchasers.

Tracking data, which monitors the progress of sales, in total, by customer group and by supplier, permits planners to assess the impact of their marketing and promotional strategies on a continuous basis.

Forecasts are essential for planning future business. Information on how markets are expected to develop in the future enables planners to assess the attraction of the market, set forward budgets and allocate marketing promotional resources in the light of the yield they could be expected to achieve. Surveys of buyers' intentions can provide a strong, though far from infallible, indication of short-term market performance. Longer-term projections rely on an analysis of trend data, the relationship between demand and general economic variables such as consumer expenditure and industrial investment and changes in taste, fashion and consumer practices.

Customer research

Customer strategies which will achieve the sales targets that have been set are a core component of marketing and promotional activity. Detailed analysis of the customer, be it an individual or an organisation, therefore represents a major task for marketing research. If, in essence, marketing is devoted to providing what the customer wants, market research is there to define **what that is**. Customer research is designed to provide marketers with an understanding of product and service requirements, customer behaviour, attitudes, purchasing preferences and purchasing procedures.

Market research is at its most valuable when assessing the potential demand for new products since this is where the unknowns are greatest and risk is high. The use of research for conceptual evaluations of customer needs and the testing of prototype designs replaces gut feel with more tangible evidence of what will or will not sell. This process extends to modifications to existing products to take account of changing customer requirements and to the definition of the services which customers require in support of their product purchases.

Only in the case of personal consumer products is the identity of the customer reasonably obvious. In most other cases, within households and most particularly within organisations, the structure of the decision making unit can be sufficiently complex to obscure the true identity of the customer. Although they may take into account the views of their peers, parents or partners, personal shoppers for clothing are generally the final decision makers when it comes to the style and colour of the items purchased and the source of supply. However, the mother buying breakfast cereal is as likely to be more influenced by the preferences of her children as her own and the father buying an automobile may take into account the requirements and preferences of the entire family. Within an organisation the buyer that places the order is normally the tip of a sizeable iceberg of individuals who contribute to the final decision. In the case of machinery purchases this can include the production management responsible for running the facility, the consultants that have helped to specify the production process, the workshop staff that will run the machines, the finance department that has to find the money to pay for it and the customers that will be expected to buy the final output. Organisational buying has long been recognised as being a complex process in which a number of staff, advisers and others can be involved (the decision making unit) each of which may be applying different buying criteria. It can also be elongated into a series of stages (the buying process) with different staff members contributing to each stage. A study by the Marketing Science Institute[1] in the USA identified eight stages in the decision making process. These are:

- anticipation and recognition of a problem and a general solution
- determination of the characteristics and quality of the needed item
- description of the characteristics and quantity of the needed items
- search for and qualification of potential sources
- acquisition and analysis of proposals
- evaluation of proposals and selection of supplier(s)
- selection of an order routine
- performance feedback and evaluation

Each of these stages can be carried out by a team whose composition varies as the process progresses and the nature of the decisions changes. The length of the process tends to vary according to whether the purchase is a repeat of previous exercises (as in the case of consumables), whether it is a completely new purchase or whether it is a modification of a previous purchasing exercise. Consumer purchasing may in principle involve the same stages but is rarely this complex. It can however, get close in the case of major items, such as cars and housing, or items on which the entire purchasing unit – the family – has strong opinions, as in the case of the annual holiday.

Research into the buying process is required to identify the individuals involved, to unravel the complexities of the interactions between them, to identify the factors which determine the choices they make and to define the mechanisms by which they reach their decisions.

Defining service strategies
The analysis of customer behaviour is most concerned with the factors that determine **customer choice of product and supplier**. Understanding the interaction between price, product quality, product features and a host of service considerations such as delivery, installation and customer advisory

services is critical to success in any marketplace. The weighting of product and supplier selection criteria shows how product and service packages should be constructed and also supplies a key input to the definition of promotional messages.

Customer satisfaction research

The drive for quality, initially expressed in programmes such as 'zero defects' aimed at ensuring that product quality was acceptable, has been transformed, largely by the introduction of the Baldridge awards in 1987, into a much broader definition of **customer satisfaction**. This takes into account not only product parameters but also the service levels that are an integral part of creating satisfied customers, such as delivery, technical support, maintenance services, responsiveness to complaints and guarantees. The promise of the brand is not just the product itself but **every point of contact** between the supplier and the customer.[2] The focus on creating a satisfied customer base was reinforced by studies which showed that it was five times more costly to gain new customers than to retain existing customers, that a 5 per cent reduction in customer losses could boost profits by between 25 per cent and 95 per cent[3] and that dissatisfied customers passed on their experience to between eight and 20 people whilst satisfied customers told only between three and five.

In order to devise and implement customer care and customer loyalty strategies it is essential to obtain a measurement of the extent to which suppliers are meeting their customers' expectations. It is equally important to demonstrate the levels of satisfaction which competitors generate with their customers. It has been shown that customers will defect to rival suppliers or rival brands even if they are highly satisfied with their current suppliers. Customer loyalty is strong only when there are strong physical barriers to change or when satisfaction exceeds that which can be provided by rival suppliers.

The growing importance of customer care and loyalty programmes has given rise to **customer satisfaction research**, which has now grown into a mainstay of the research business and supports a number of specialist suppliers. **Image research**, once far more popular, is closely allied in that it shows customers' perceptions of suppliers. Perceptions can be equally as powerful as reality in determining supplier acceptance and research can highlight changes in image and performance which need to be engineered in order to improve the chances of success.

Customer satisfaction surveys have three key elements:

- a listing of the **product and service attributes** which customers use to evaluate the performance of their suppliers
- ratings which shows customers' **perceptions of suppliers' performance** on each product and service attribute
- a rating of **overall satisfaction** with the supplier.

Since not all attributes are of equal importance to customers, the quality of the measurement is enhanced if the attributes are also given an importance weighting. The survey can be further improved by asking for explanations for poor ratings, testing the loyalty of the consumer to the supplier and seeking information on the extent to which consumers will recommend suppliers to third parties. A customer satisfaction survey may contain measurements of awareness, on the grounds that suppliers who have low levels of awareness outside their existing customer base are unlikely to gain market share, however much satisfaction they are capable of delivering.

Responses to the overall satisfaction question are particularly valuable when analysing the reasons **why** a supplier is successful. Regression analysis relating the perceived performance on each attribute with overall satisfaction can be used to identify the key drivers of satisfaction. Tabulations which contrast required or stated performance (the importance weightings) with derived satisfaction (the results of the regression analysis) normally highlight some interesting conclusions for market planners. One of these is usually that some factors which respondents claim are highly important do not in practice influence their behaviour. Surveys of venture capital users repeatedly show that the most important aspect of the service they seek is a deal made on favourable terms to themselves. Customer satisfaction research shows that they nevertheless use suppliers of venture capital who offer them terms which they regard as adverse. Stated importance and derived importance are clearly opposed to each other.

Simpler inferences from customer satisfaction surveys can be drawn from **gap analysis**, which relates performance to importance. Though valuable, this does not address the frequent differences between what respondents say and what they do.

Another refinement to customer satisfaction research is the inclusion of a measurement of the performance of competitors. At its simplest, the use of competitive measurements acknowledges that relative performance is just as important as the absolute level of performance. Excellent performance may not be good enough in a market containing a number of stars. Mediocre performance may be good enough to succeed (at least temporarily) if the other suppliers are poor. Relative performance is particularly important when perceptions of quality and value are included in the mix. According to Bradley Gale, 'Quality means little in business unless customers perceive your quality as superior to your competitors'.[4]

Pricing research
Price, and value, are central to customer satisfaction and research exercises are frequently required to grapple with issues such as the actual prices being paid, discounts received, the optimum prices for products or services and the level of price sensitivity which exists in markets. Despite its importance, marketing research texts are surprisingly silent on the subject of pricing research. Continuous and ad hoc studies concentrate on prices actually paid

for products and discounts and other incentives received, but marketing strategists, particularly those handling new products, require data which predicts the prices they can achieve for their products. Modelling techniques, which predict consumer choice at alternative price levels, go some way to providing this data but one of the most valuable tools, the **price sensitivity meter** developed by the Dutch Statistical Institute, is still almost unique as a simple predictor of price levels.[5]

Marketing or brand equity measurement
The long-term consequence of an investment in marketing is the establishment of an equity position which can be measured either at the level of the brand or the total marketing equity that the company has built-up (see Box 4.4). The equity consists of the **recognition** of a company name or brand and the **values** that are attached to it. Recognition represents an obvious benefit since customers generally prefer to do business with companies they know or have at least heard of, rather than those which are unknown. Recognition provides the consumer with comfort that the product will be of an acceptable quality level. It will also ensure that the product is on the list of those that will be considered for purchase. This will commonly result in a recognised brand name generating more income than an unknown or less well known brand. But on its own, recognition is not enough.

The intangible attributes or values that are attached to the name are equally important in that they also increase the level of acceptance of the company as a supplier. Customers buy brands not just because of the features they offer but also because they wish to associate with the **intangible benefits the brand offers**. The true difference between Mercedes and BMW

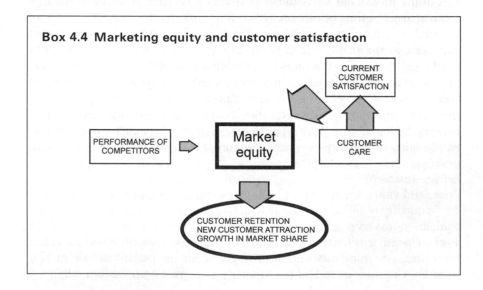

Box 4.4 Marketing equity and customer satisfaction

may lie as much in the images the brands create as in the performance of their vehicles.

A strong brand or marketing equity position permits companies to improve the reach of their marketing budgets and charge price premiums. A strong brand can also overcome quality problems – at least for a while. This contrasts with brands which have a poor equity position and have to pedal that much harder in order to achieve sales. Rover, prior to its acquisition by BMW, fell into the latter category. Building an equity position is particularly important to suppliers of non-differentiated products. Until loyalty schemes were developed, oil companies spent considerable sums on building their brand position as one of the relatively few means they had of capturing and retaining their market share.

A key aspect of marketing equity is that it is divorced from the current marketing activities of suppliers, though these may add to or detract from the equity stock. Differences in marketing equity can explain why companies which are operating strong marketing programmes still find it difficult to gain market share from less vigorous but older established competitors. The marketing equity pattern does not necessarily distinguish between companies that had strong names in the past and are living off their reputations and those that are on their way up and are carving new reputations. The difference is analogous to that between those which are expending considerable energy to peddle uphill and those which are coasting downhill. Although these two organisational types will drift apart, at any point in time they may have equally strong equity positions. For most suppliers their marketing equity represents a substantial part of their overall marketing assets, but it needs to be quantified and understood if it is to be used effectively. The strength of the asset can be assessed not only by measuring its content but also by observing the extent to which it matches the **real requirements of customers**.

Market segmentation

Customer research is commonly used to define discrete segments of a market which lend themselves to separate marketing approaches. It is rarely easy to be all things to all people and marketing effectiveness can be improved by targeting specific market segments with the products, services and marketing messages they find most acceptable. Segments can be defined by parameters such as geography, demographics, taste, attitudes and buying practices but research is required to show whether the segments are sufficiently different and homogeneous to support separate marketing approaches.[6]

Purchasing intentions

Research into customers' purchasing intentions is used to compute short-term forecasts of demand for products and to predict the success of new products. The accuracy of the results tends to be higher in industrial and professional markets where there is a close correlation between stated purchasing intentions and actual behaviour, but surveys of consumer purchasing intentions can also provide a valuable input to short-term forecasting models.

Communications research

The study of the effectiveness of individual marketing communication and promotional techniques provides planners with guidelines for the allocation of their marketing expenditure. The research is usually divided into pre-testing and post-testing. **Pre-testing** seeks to establish which of a series of alternatives is likely to work best in terms of its impact and the effectiveness with which it communicates the desired message. **Post-testing** seeks to establish whether the campaign actually worked. Pre-testing involves an in-depth analysis of the reactions of small samples of potential customers. **Post-testing** is carried out with larger samples of customers and potential customers that have been exposed to the campaigns.

The effectiveness of advertising, direct marketing, sales promotion, exhibitions, public relations and sponsorship is usually studied indirectly by testing awareness, the number of column inches achieved, recall and customers' reaction to content such as copy, images and venues. The real effectiveness of advertising – namely, the effect on income – is more difficult to establish, though a number of models are available to compute the relationship between advertising expenditure and sales. The effectiveness of below-the-line expenditure (direct marketing and sales promotion) is normally apparent in the form of response and take-up rates arising from specific campaigns, and does not normally need to be established by research.

The most complex research relates to communications activities which are designed to influence but are not expected to yield immediate contacts or feed through directly to sales. The effectiveness of sponsorship is particularly difficult to gauge. Whilst the reactions of those that are invited to participate in the corporate hospitality which commonly accompanies sponsorship is measurable, the effect on wider audiences of the posters advertising the name of the sponsor, the programme notes, the decals on sponsored vehicles or logos on sportswear may be too subtle to be picked up by any research other than that designed to measure awareness. There are glaring exceptions to this observation, such as the London Rubber Company's pre-AIDS use of Formula One racing car sponsorship in order to circumvent the ban on conventional advertising of condoms that was then in force.[7]

The problems with measuring the effectiveness of sponsorship arise from the fact that it is both designed and perceived as being more altruistic than advertising. As such, its commercial effect is blunted and while it is possible to determine whether sponsors are viewed more favourably as a result of their patronage, the link to purchasing is more difficult to establish.

Media research

Media research is an important component of communications research which is devoted to analysing newspaper and journal readership, radio and television audiences, poster viewing and cinema audiences. To be fully effective media research should be allied with research into purchasing decision making, so that the relationship between those responsible for purchase decisions and media audiences can be demonstrated.

Other aspects of marketing activity which can be pre- and post-tested by studying customer reactions include the use and effectiveness of distribution channels, packaging and merchandising.

Channel research

A high proportion of products flow from supplier to customer through various types of distributor. The attitudes, practices and requirements of the operators of distribution channels can therefore have a significant effect on supplier performance. In many markets a failure on the part of distributors to stock, display or merchandise products will undermine all other marketing programmes.

Channel research can probe all aspects of distributors' operations and requirements to provide a basis for the development of effective distribution strategies (Box 4.5).

Box 4.5 The key channel decisions

The key channel decisions relate to which channels to use and how they can be motivated and the types of information which can support these decisions include:

- identifying the **channels operating** in each segment of a market and a measurement of their **relative importance**
- examining the **segments of the markets** serviced by each distributor
- measuring **channel catchment areas**
- defining the **requirements of distributors** from suppliers in order to induce them to stock and promote products
- identifying **channel margin requirements** and the tasks they are prepared to undertake
- examining the **range of products** stocked by distributors and the shelf space allocated to products and brands
- testing the relationship between channel owners and product suppliers, notably its **duration**, the **basis on which it exists** and the conditions under which it could be **broken**
- testing the effectiveness with which channels implement the **service and promotional strategies** of suppliers.

Competitor intelligence

The widespread adoption of customer research by suppliers of consumer and industrial products and suppliers of professional services has resulted in noticeable similarities in product and service strategies. Reductions in differentiation in customer strategies has heightened interest in competitor strategies which are aimed at improving or defending market share. Interest in competitive strategies was also boosted by a number of authors in the 1980s who wrote on the subject of 'marketing warfare' and competition. These pointed out that as market growth slowed, the level of competition in markets was destined to increase and that managers therefore needed to learn how to attack their opponents and defend themselves. The authors (Kotler and Singh,[8] Porter,[9] Ries and Trout[10] and Duro and Sandstrom[11]) all pointed out that competitive marketing could learn many lessons from military strategies and tactics.

In order to compete it is essential not only to identify the competition but also to understand their resources, their strategies, their strengths and weaknesses as perceived by customers, the threat they pose to other suppliers and their vulnerabilities to attack. Detailed knowledge of competitors has never been easy to acquire and marketing history is littered with examples of successful businesses that have been brought down by competition which was either unknown or known but undervalued. There are also countless examples of opportunities missed through failures to capitalise on competitors' weaknesses.

Keeping abreast of competition is becoming increasingly difficult as the pace of change in markets accelerates. Competitive tension is being heightened by powerful forces which are driving existing competitors to

---

Box 4.6 Competitor information profile

A typical competitor information profile will cover:

- ownership and organisational structure
- financial history
- financial resources
- key decision makers and their track records
- staff resources
- production resources and locations
- product lines and portfolios
- patents, licences and other unique assets
- markets and segments serviced
- distribution channels used
- export activity and countries supplied
- sales and marketing activities.

be more aggressive and at the same time opening markets to new competitors. Deregulation, reductions in trade barriers, radical political realignments and the increasing globalisation of supply all create new opportunities but at the same time threaten those who fail to appreciate that the competitive environment is changing and that previous competitive boundaries have been blurred or eliminated.

The most basic information requirement is a map which plots the competitive environment and shows who the competitors are, where they are, where they have come from and the resources they deploy.

The profile can be extended by probing each competitor's image, reputation, strengths and weaknesses among customers.

4.3 Marketing Tasks and Market Information Requirements

Box 4.7 shows the types of market information that can contribute to the common marketing tasks identified above.

4.4 Ancillary Information

Information obtained from direct participants in the marketplace is sometimes insufficient to solve a marketing problem and the support of data derived from other sources is required. The groups that are most commonly analysed include:

- employees and other stakeholders in companies
- market influences – individuals whose position or activities enable them to influence the performance of markets and companies.

Information derived from employees and other stakeholders

Although the analysis of customers dominates market research activity, there is growing use of techniques to examine the attitudes and requirements of the management and staff of companies. This research is commonly extended to cover shareholders, bankers and other stakeholders in businesses. The neutrality of a research-based approach is recognised as offering significant advantages when probing what are often highly sensitive subjects.

Internal research may be a logical counterpart to external market research as well as being used to support internal management decisions. The level of **employee loyalty** is almost as important to companies as customer loyalty, in that it can have a significant effect on operational efficiency and costs.

Box 4.7 Marketing tasks and information requirements

Marketing task	Information requirement
New product development	Total sales, Sales by product category, Reaction to proposed product features
New product launches	Monitor test marketing programmes
Expansion of production capacity	Total sales, Analysis of market structure, Projections of market growth, Competitor analysis
Re-launches of existing products	Analysis of customer requirements, Customer satisfaction research
Segmentation strategies	Analysis of sales by key segmentation criteria – e.g. Customer type or geographical region
Distribution/ marketing channel strategies	Sales by distribution channel, Analysis of requirements of distributors, Research into distributors' margin requirements, Mystery shopping exercises
Sales strategies	Analysis of buyer decision making processes, Analysis of the decision making unit, Communications research, Analysis of customer information requirements, Analysis of competitors' sales methods
Service strategies	Analysis of customer service requirements
Customer care programmes	Analysis of customer service requirements, Customer satisfaction research
Pricing strategies	Analysis of prevailing prices in the market, Analysis of the sensitivity of customers to price
Brand development	Brand strengths of competing products, Image of specific brands
Packaging	Analysis of customer packaging requirements, Packaging methods used by competitors, Tests of new packaging on customers
Advertising and promotional programmes	Pre-tests of advertising copy and images, Recall of supplier advertising
Awareness and image campaigns	Test awareness of suppliers, Measurement of attitudes towards products and suppliers
Competitive strategies	Analysis of competitive suppliers' products, Marketing programmes, Resources and strategies
Export marketing strategies	Analysis of size structure and trends of export markets, Customer expectation research, Analysis of customer satisfaction, Analysis of competitor activities in export markets, Analysis of local standards and regulations

Employee awareness is also a key factor. For example, customer care strategies commonly require internal programmes to educate employees on the service requirements of customers. The development of these programmes benefits considerably from information which shows employees' current perceptions of customer needs. The resultant information can then be compared with actual customer requirements to show any significant divergences which require correction.

Employee satisfaction research is used to provide a barometer of industrial relations and to highlight potential changes in management, benefits and remuneration packages which will improve productivity and reduce staff turnover. Such research may also be used to test employee reaction to proposed changes before they are implemented and in a way which does not imply that they are already part of corporate policy.

Employee communications surveys are used to test the effectiveness of communication channels within companies by testing the accuracy of information held by employees and employee reaction to communication methods that are deployed.

Research among shareholders, particularly the powerful institutional shareholders, is used to test reactions to management policy or to major proposed changes, such as mergers, acquisitions or divestments. The opinions of shareholders and their advisors, such as stockbrokers, are significant in that they can seriously affect the value of the company through movements in share prices.

Information derived from market influencers

Business strategy can be influenced by a number of groups which fall outside the customer, distributor, competitor and employee categories outlined above. They include politicians, journalists, bankers, pressure groups and others whose actions and opinions can have a direct or indirect influence on the performance of markets and suppliers. Direct action includes the framing of legislation, such as restrictions on advertising, which hampers companies' ability to promote their products. Indirect action includes the shaping of public opinion in such a way that specific products, services or company actions become less acceptable. Some markets, particularly those which relate to health or the environment, are highly vulnerable to external influences. Shell's image will take many years to recover from the high profile campaign mounted by Greenpeace against the offshore disposal of the Brent Spar oil rig, even though the facts used by Greenpeace were subsequently shown to be innaccurate and submerged structures have been found to enhance marine life rather than threaten it. Research carried out among opinion formers can identify attitudes towards specific issues which are likely to be projected to a wider audience and can provide key inputs to strategy, such as the likely timing of restrictive legislation.

4.5 **Responsibility for Defining Information Needs**

The marketing information needs of an organisation should be defined by those that will use the results. This means that all those involved in the development and implementation of marketing strategies and tactical marketing programmes should have an input, depending on the precise nature of the problem. Unfortunately, as the number of people involved in the definition of information requirements increases so does the number of questions and therefore the scale of the research programme. Furthermore, those who need use research data are not always well versed in what market research programmes can achieve. Clearly, to maintain control, one person should assume responsibility for defining needs, but should do so by conferring with those that will use the information. It will also help if that person has some familiarity with market research.

In large, regular users of research this person is likely to be the market research or business intelligence manager whose role, in addition to information specification, will include:

- liaison with information users
- specification of research methods
- completion of in-house research exercises
- selection of external information sources
- control of external surveys
- verification of research findings
- interpretation of findings for management.

In smaller organisations with sporadic research needs the appointment of a full-time research manager is rarely justified and the task of coordinating surveys falls to one of those that will use the information. A wide diversity of job functions can fill this role, depending on who is available and the importance attached to the outcome. In the case of surveys designed to support major strategic decisions the chief executive, marketing director or planning director may play a central role. In the case of less prominent exercises the task may fall to the:

- business development manager
- marketing manager
- marketing services manager
- sales manager
- advertising manager
- product manager
- brand manager.

If, as is commonly the case, an outside research agency is to be used to collect market information, they too should be consulted as part of the information specification process. Their expertise on the types of information that it is feasible to collect, the cost of information collection and the timescales required will provide a valuable counterpoint to internal opinions on what is required.

Whoever assumes the role of specifying the information needed, the key requirement is consultation with other users to ensure that the coverage is complete and that all parties **'buy-into' the findings**. Unpopular research findings can be too easily dismissed by those that can claim that they had no involvement in the preparatory stages of the research.

Notes

1 Patrick J. Robinson and Charles W. Farris, *Industrial Buying and Creative Marketing* (Boston, Allyn & Bacon Inc., 1967).
2 'A Satisfied Customer Isn't Enough', *Fortune* (July 21 1997), pp. 112–13.
3 'Why Some Customers are More Equal than Others', *Fortune* (September 19 1994), pp. 215–24.
4 Bradley T. Gale, *Managing Customer Value* (New York, Free Press, 1994).
5 Peter van Westendorp, 'NSS Price Sensitivity Meter (PSM): A New Approach to Study Consumer Perception of Prices', EMSOMAR Paper.
6 For a fuller discussion of market segmentation, see Chapter 8.
7 See A. Wilson and C. West, 'The Marketing of Unmentionables', *Harvard Business Review* (January–February 1981).
8 P. Kotler and R. Singh, 'Marketing Warfare in the 1980s', *The Journal of Business Strategy* (Winter 1981).
9 Michael Porter, *Competitive Strategy* (New York, Free Press, 1980).
10 Al Ries and Jack Trout, *Marketing Warfare* (New York, McGraw-Hill, 1986).
11 Robert Duro and Bjorn Sandstrom, *The Basic Principles of Marketing Warfare* (Chichester, John Wiley, 1987).

5 Structure of Research Activity

In order to fully understand the research services that are available it is necessary to understand how research activity is structured. Where once this was simple it is now complex. There are few professions – indeed, there are few businesses – which do not, amoeba-like, fragment themselves into increasingly specialised segments, and market research is no exception. Just as the general legal practitioner has been increasingly marginalised by those who specialise in divorce, conveyancing, corporate, marine or patent law, the market research business is made up of a series of specialisations which have become increasingly distinct from each other in terms of what they do and the methods they use. The divisions reflect the different characteristics of the markets studied, the wide variety of market information that is required, the speed at which it is needed, the proliferation of research techniques and the applications for the information. The organisations or research techniques best suited to one problem may be totally inappropriate for another, even though they may appear superficially similar.

The main factors which determine the structure of research activity are:

- research purpose
- research approach
- type of market
- type of survey

5.1 Research Purpose

Research problems can be categorised according to whether the user of the data is seeking to **explore the** nature of a market or whether there is a need to **describe** the patterns which exist. The terms 'exploratory' and 'descriptive' tend to overlap with **qualitative** and **quantitative** research.

Exploratory research

Exploratory research is carried out when knowledge levels are low and there is insufficient information to structure the problem. It is commonly required in the case of new products, when market conditions are changing rapidly and the past is no longer an accurate guide to the future, and when the research user is examining a market which is completely unfamiliar.

Box 5.1 Exploratory research for marketing

Typical examples of exploratory research for marketing are:

- defining the **characteristics required** in new products
- understanding the factors which determine the ways in which markets are **segmented**
- understanding the **decision making process**
- defining the criteria by which customers **select** the products they purchase
- identifying the criteria by which customers **evaluate** the performance of suppliers.

Exploratory research is concerned with **issues and behaviour** rather than statistics, and is closely associated with the more creative marketing functions, particularly new product development (Box 5.1).

Descriptive research

Descriptive research is used to **profile and structure** the marketplace in terms of demand volumes, customer segments, product use, distribution channels used, customer attitudes, prices paid and media readership. It results in hard statistical data rather than the softer material provided by exploratory research.

Qualitative and quantitative research

The terms exploratory and descriptive research are less frequently used in the market research business than **qualitative** and **quantitative** research.

Qualitative research techniques are used primarily in exploratory research where there is a requirement to understand, explore, diagnose, generate ideas, test hypotheses and gain insight into a market situation. It is normal used early on in the knowledge building process, though it can be applied when there is a need to gain further understanding once a quantitative survey has been completed. Qualitative research uses in-depth techniques and by its nature, is rarely carried out with large samples.

In contrast, **quantitative** research is used to describe the marketplace and the patterns which exist within it. It is commonly large-scale research based on substantial samples. It is highly mechanical in its approach, relying on statistical interpretation, rather than the intuition that forms the basis of qualitative analyses.

Qualitative research often precedes quantitative research and provides the basis for questionnaire development. However, the sequence is not inevitable since many problems can be solved entirely by a qualitative research approach and market structures may be well enough understood to initiate a quantitative survey without first building a model of customer behaviour by means of a qualitative exercise.

The terms 'qualitative' and 'quantitative' are important to remember since research companies use them to describe the services they offer. There is little point in approaching a qualitative research company for a descriptive, quantitative survey and vice versa.

5.2 **Research Approach**

Market research is most commonly associated with a survey approach requiring significant samples to generate quantitative information. However, in addition to the qualitative exercises described above, the research business has also had to cope with situations in which sample surveys are impractical, would take too long to complete or would cost too much. As a result **survey research** is complemented by **business intelligence** and **competitive intelligence** as approaches which can be equally valid sources of information for business decision making even though they do not use the disciplines of a survey approach.

Survey research

Survey research involves the systematic application of representative sampling, questionnaire design, information collection and statistical analysis techniques to obtain data which describes aspects of a market in as much detail required by the research user. The size of the sample is determined by a combination of factors including the structure of the market being examined, the level of detail required and the accuracy levels required. Together these will determine whether a large or relatively small survey is required, and therefore the overall cost of the research.

By definition, surveys are **descriptive**. The full range of data they can provide has been set out in full in Chapter 4 but in essence they include measurements of all of the parameters of a market required to define a marketing strategy, including the characteristics of customers, product ownership, product use, purchases, source of purchase, purchasing procedures, awareness, attitudes and recall of marketing communications.

The primary targets of most market surveys are **customers** – those whose requirements, practices and attitudes determine the marketing strategies that are adopted. However, surveys are also used to obtain data from a variety of other individuals and organisations that can influence what is purchased and thereby play a role in the marketing process. These include:

- distributors (retail and wholesale)
- designers
- specifiers.

Survey research has a number of applications in addition to market analysis. Academic research, social research and opinion polling are the most prominent and whilst these have little in common with commercial market research they have been responsible for advances in research techniques and their results can contribute to the understanding of customers.

Business intelligence

Business intelligence is an alternative method of obtaining market information which uses primary data collection techniques but directs them at limited numbers of concentrated or highly informed sources rather than significant samples of customers or distributors (Box 5.2).

Business intelligence exercises can cover all aspects of business operations and the tasks range from a relatively straightforward profile of the product ranges of competitive suppliers by analysing catalogues to the provision of complex details on the structure of a company's production and distribution resources.

In general, a business intelligence approach is better suited to the provision of data on how markets or suppliers work rather than customer information. However, where a market includes a number of key accounts, such as major wholesalers or retailers or large corporate buyers, the provision of information on their activities may be an appropriate business intelligence objective.

The direct nature of business intelligence can make it a difficult approach to adopt. The primary skills that are required are:

- an ability to **identify sources** that possess the information required
- the ability to make sources **disclose** the information they possess.

Very often, the most obvious sources or those which are easiest to identify are also the most difficult to question and the two skills therefore tend to compensate for each other. For example, the most obvious source of details on a company's manufacturing resources would be the production director but there are no obvious reasons why he would reveal these to a third party

---

Box 5.2 Key characteristics of business intelligence

The key characteristics are that:

- its information objectives are generally more limited than a market survey
- the information obtained may be subject to a wider range of error
- there is less certainty that the information will be obtained
- it can be quick to apply
- it can cost less than sample surveys.

enquirer and it would take a highly persuasive approach to encourage him to do so. Customers or affiliates of the company may possess some information on manufacturing resources and are easier to talk to. Unfortunately, they are also substantially more difficult to identify.

Competitive intelligence

Competitive intelligence is a research objective which has matured into being a research specialisation in its own right. It is defined as 'a systematic programme for gathering and analysing information about competitors'.[1] Its growth has been driven by a requirement for data to support competitive strategies which are increasingly independent of marketing strategies. Although competition has always been a fundamental characteristic of markets, suppliers have tended to rely on product, service or price superiority in order to grow or defend their market shares. This has become progressively more difficult as product designs have tended to converge and it has become increasingly difficult to maintain a level of true differentiation between suppliers. The process has been exacerbated in recession or periods of slow growth when individual suppliers can grow their sales only at the expense of their competitors.

As set out in Chapter 4 (p. 34), this can be likened to 'war' and in wartime it is essential to:

- **identify** the opposing forces
- **analyse** their resources, strengths and weaknesses
- understand their **objectives, missions and strategies**
- **survey** the territory that they hold and are defending
- **anticipate** their tactics
- define the strategies and tactics by which they can be **overcome**.

Some of these objectives can be achieved by survey and business intelligence approaches but others require a specific intelligence approach. For example, customer satisfaction surveys can be designed to yield information on the strengths and weaknesses of competitive suppliers and consumer panel data will provide the demographics of a competitor's customer base. However, to define a competitor's strategy in the market-place requires information which cannot be obtained from customers though it might be available from statements made by the company itself, by analysing the characteristics of the company's management and their previous track records or from those whose business it is to analyse companies' performance, such as the analysts working in stockbrokers.

Whilst the techniques used for competitive intelligence are similar to those used for survey research, the sources of information are not. In some instances, this raises questions of research ethics. The borderline between competitor intelligence and industrial espionage could be perceived as being a fine one. In practice, this should not be the case; whereas in industrial espionage any technique is acceptable, including theft, competitor intelligence is founded on the principle that no illegal act is committed and no deception is used in order to obtain the required information. This places constraints on what can be achieved but also yields a premium for those that have the ingenuity and the analytical skills to obtain results within ethical boundaries (see Chapter 21).

5.3 **Type of Market**

A key division in research activity is created by the type of market studied. In general terms markets can be classified into consumer and industrial, the latter including corporate, institutional and government markets.

Consumer markets

By far the highest proportion of research expenditure is spent on the analysis of consumer markets. Consumer markets are comprised of the millions of individuals resident in each country who purchase for their personal needs, for the needs of their families or for their friends. The purchases are primarily consumer products such as food, personal items, durables and consumer services. Whilst need and affordability are primary drivers of demand, product selection is also based on a host of less tangible and less predictable factors, such as fashion, recognition and self-esteem.

A high proportion of consumer products are purchased regularly and the markets can change rapidly and be subject to fierce levels of competition using the full armoury of promotional techniques. Where mass marketing is involved, the profits from success are high – but so are risks of failure. It is a climate in which the benefits of knowledge can be all too readily appreciated.

The characteristic of consumer markets which makes research an acceptable insurance policy to suppliers is their scale. Customers can commonly be measured in millions and even minority markets can run to hundreds of thousands of purchasers. Monitoring customer activities, sounding opinions, establishing requirements and testing preferences on this scale by anything other than a significant survey is highly risky. This contrasts strongly with many industrial markets which, as described below, may contain relatively few buyers all of whom could be well known to suppliers.

Consumer universes are large but can be relatively simply segmented. Although in an attempt to make messages more highly personalised there is a trend towards refining the marketing process so that it reaches out to smaller and smaller customer segments, there are relatively few homogeneous classifications into which all customers fall. Market segments can be defined by age and sex, by geographical region, by need, by socio-economic group and by type of residence, but even the largest of these (residences) creates only 50–60 separate segmentations.

Industrial, professional, institutional and government markets

In industrial, professional, institutional and government markets purchasing is for organisational use rather than the satisfaction of individual needs. Decisions are still made by people but with their working hats on. The markets themselves are considerably more complex than those for consumer products and services and the risks attached to poor decision making are as high, if not higher. The number of orders placed may be relatively few and customers may buy infrequently, but average order sizes can be many thousands of times bigger than those encountered in consumer markets.

The main causes of complexity in industrial markets lie in the fact that specifying and purchasing are rarely in the hands of a single individual and the criteria by which suppliers are selected and evaluated take into account a wide range of technical and commercial considerations as well as the emotional factors that operate so powerfully in consumer markets. Buyers of industrial products have a heightened need to be seen to have made a good decision as their jobs are at stake as well as their professional esteem. All of this points to an increased need for market analysis to provide marketing and sales staff with a firm foundation for decisions.

The complexity of industrial markets can be offset by the fact that the number of potential customers is a fraction of the customer base for consumer products. There are exceptions such as office equipment and telecommunications equipment, which are sold into very large industrial universes, but the norm is small customer bases in which it is theoretically easier to gain in-depth knowledge of customer practices and requirements. An industrial sales force calling regularly on clients can be easily persuaded that it understands the market in which it is operating. This is rarely true and any sense of complete understanding is usually misplaced.

Although they contain considerably fewer customers, industrial, professional and institutional markets segment into many more groupings. The broad bands of homogeneity observed in consumer markets can be virtually non-existent, sometimes to the point where the requirements of each customer is unique. A combination of the production processes used, the design of the products produced, geographical location, the size of the orders placed and the characteristics of the personnel involved in decision making can necessitate marketing approaches which differ significantly from one industrial client to another.

Sector specialisation

Despite the complexities of industrial markets, the use of marketing research to profile customers' requirements is the exception rather than the rule. The organisation which do make extensive use research, sometimes on the scale witnessed amongst the manufacturers of consumer products, tend to be active in businesses in which market conditions are changing rapidly, where the risks are extremely high, where competition is severe and where there is a heavy use of marketing and promotional techniques. A number of these sectors are 'consumer-like' in that there are large numbers of customers with broadly similar requirements, such as doctors, farmers and office managers. Specialist research services have been developed to meet the needs of these sectors and prominent amongst them are research services designed specifically for the pharmaceutical, healthcare, chemical and packaging industries.

5.4 Type of Survey

The type of survey is a further differentiator of research services (Box 5.3).

Box 5.3 Survey types

Six different survey types are available each with its own characteristics and benefits to the research user. In broadly descending order of importance they are:

- Panel surveys
- Retail audits
- Ad hoc surveys
- Omnibus surveys
- Syndicated research
- Published research.

Panels

Panels of customers can either be **continuous** or **standing**. Continuous panels are used to collect information regularly, normally month by month, from customers selected to represent all households, specific groups of individuals or organisations. Panel members are recruited to provide information on a regular basis and one of their primary advantages is that they facilitate the tracking of trends over long periods of time. The most widely used panels are those which are made up of households or individual consumers. These are best suited to the collection of information on purchases that are made regularly and record simple data, such as products or services purchased, the source of purchase, prices paid and the receipt of any incentives or special offers with the purchase.

The continuous panel technique has also been used amongst businesses and professionals where panels of wholesalers, manufacturing companies, operators of transport fleets, office managers, hospitals and doctors have provided regular information on their output, forward orders, business confidence and purchases.

Standing panels are much larger than continuous panels and comprise individuals or households who have agreed to participate in surveys as and when required. Demographic and product ownership data is held on each panel member. Standing panels are large enough to represent not only the consumer universe as a whole but also all types of minority groups, such as families with infants, owners of specific types of automobile or households equipped with PCs. The panel is rarely used in its entirety but as a source of samples which are drawn according to the particular requirements of the product or service being studied. The oldest of these panels is run by NFO in the USA and consists of 550,000 households.

The most widespread use of panel research is monitoring expenditure on regular purchases where there is intense competition for market share and, among media, for advertising revenues. The earliest examples were developed to track expenditure on packaged groceries and for measuring the audiences for television programmes (such as the British Audience Research Bureau (BARB) programme in the UK and the Nielsen National Television Index in the USA). In non-consumer markets the most durable examples of panel research are the IMS hospital and doctor panels which report on drug prescriptions and purchases of hospital supplies and equipment. Panels are also valuable for monitoring developments in markets which are changing rapidly, such as financial services, telecommunications and information technology. In these markets new entrants and companies launching new products need continuous research data showing the impact of their marketing programmes in terms of awareness levels and the uptake of their products or services.

The recruitment and maintenance of panels is an expensive business which means that there tend to be relatively few of them in each country and their operators need to work them hard in order to recoup their investment. They are viable only when the resultant data is sold to large numbers of clients. The data that is collected is used for the preparation of standard reports and also as an input to special analyses, which are prepared when clients have requirements which go beyond the contents of the standard reports.

Retail audits

Retail auditing is used to collect data which is similar to that recorded by continuous consumer panels, but the source of the data is a sample of retail outlets rather than customers. Electronic data collection techniques using point of sale data are moving retail research more towards censuses than samples, though not all retailers in a sector are prepared to cooperate with research agencies. Clearly what passes through retail outlets should agree with purchases made by customers and the main differences between consumer panel and retail audit data lie in the ways in which the data can be structured and analysed.

Retail audits and consumer panels are both used to provide quantitative information which tracks purchasing trends. Neither seek information which explain the trends which are observed. Both achieve high degrees of accuracy and produce detailed information by covering large samples of respondents or a high proportion of outlets.

Ad hoc

Ad hoc surveys cope with research requirements which arise sporadically and which cannot be satisfied adequately by panel or syndicated research. Each survey is custom-designed to meet specific information needs or to solve any of a wide variety of marketing problems. The main advantage of ad hoc surveys is that the client obtains the precise information that is required and retains proprietary control over it. Panel and retail audit data can be customised by means of special analysis, which is also the proprietary property of the client that commissions it, but the amount of tailoring that can be achieved is limited by the type and structure of the initial data that is collected.

Omnibus surveys

Omnibus surveys are regular research exercises carried out weekly, monthly or quarterly with defined samples of respondents such as motorists, mothers with young children or general samples representative of the population as a whole. Clients use omnibus surveys as a vehicle for carrying questions they want answered but which do not justify the cost of a specially mounted ad hoc survey. An omnibus questionnaire can carry 2–3 questions from 10–15 separate clients. Each client receives an analysis of the responses to the questions they have placed and pays a fee for each question asked.

Syndicated

Syndicated or multi-client surveys are research programmes for which the cost is shared by a group of clients who wish to participate. Shared cost means that clients gain the benefit of research programmes many times larger than they could afford on their own. The disadvantage is that competitors have access to the same data, but this may be justified by the savings in cost. Syndicates can either be 'closed', meaning that a predetermined group of clients buys the research and no further sale is permitted, or 'open', meaning that anyone can buy the research.

The term 'multi-client surveys' is generally applied to major pieces of research for which the subscription prices are high. They are often set up and promoted by research companies but they may also be initiated by groups of companies or by trade associations acting on behalf of their members.

Published research

Published research can be viewed as the poor man's version of syndicated studies. Normally available at relatively low prices, the reports seek to provide basic descriptions of markets and are derived from limited research programmes. Their main use is for initial market orientation rather than a platform for product or marketing strategies. Published research is available from a wide range of publishers who select topics either on the basis of what they feel will sell or because they lie within the specific area of expertise of the sponsoring organisation.

5.5 Obtaining Information

Two basic options exist for obtaining information:

- use **in-house research resources** to collect it, interpret it and present it to management
- **purchase data from vendors** who specialise in its collection and interpretation.

If in-house research resources exist there is always a strong case for using them unless it is imperative that the research is not associated with the commissioning company, the task is too large to be handled by the resources available, special research skills or techniques which are not available internally are required or it is essential that the results are seen to be free of any internal biases.

Throughout the world there is a prolific supply of market research consultants capable of obtaining all types of data that could conceivably be required. The market research industry has responded to the information requirements of its clients in a variety of ways, each reflecting the difficulty and cost of acquiring the information and the extent to which clients require information which is proprietary to themselves or are prepared to share it with others. The divisions in the research business and the specialisations of each company broadly reflect the types of research activity described in this chapter.

Notes

1 Larry Kahaner, *Competitive Intelligence: From Black Ops to Boardrooms – How to Gather, Analyse and Use Information to Succeed in the Global Marketplace* (New York, Simon & Schuster, 1996).

6 Internal and Secondary Information Sources

The lowest-cost information is normally that which has already been collected internally or has been published by external organisations. It also has the advantage of being available quickly. Internal and secondary information sources will never meet all information needs, but they can be important and should never be overlooked.

6.1 Internal Research

All companies have access to information on their markets. This will have been acquired over time and by a variety of methods (Box 6.1).

Box 6.1 Sources of information

The most common sources are:

- **Human intelligence**
  - the experience of company staff
  - staff who have previously worked for competitors
  - field sales reports
  - reports from distributors.

- **Company records and documents**
  - accounts records
  - sales analyses
  - customer databases
  - internal collections of trade journals press reports and statistics
  - previously commissioned market reports.

Human intelligence

The most valuable information can reside in the heads of the **company's own staff**. Its value derives from the fact that it has been gained by experience, either with the current or previous employers, and that it can provide qualitative insight into a market which is rarely available from company records and statistics. The information available from human sources can cover:

- **events** (such as new products, new competitors, changes of distributor or personnel changes)
- **performance information** (such as business gains and losses, reasons for lost business)
- **customer information** (typically customers' or distributors' requirements from suppliers and customers' reported satisfaction with suppliers).

The information can be categorised as facts, rumours and guesswork and the greatest danger in the use of human intelligence is that the **rumours and guesswork are treated as facts**.

Staff who have direct contact with customers, distributors and competitors are best placed to obtain and absorb information and new recruits who have previously worked for competitors can often provide particularly interesting perspectives on a market. **De-briefing recruits about their previous companies** is a standard procedure in many companies, but needs to be handled carefully to ensure that no ethical boundaries are crossed. Absorbing the experience and intellectual property that a staff member has acquired by virtue of previous employment is a legitimate activity and may be a key reason why a particular individual was employed; however, it can go too far in that the individual may be expected to provide information which is seriously detrimental to the interests of the previous employer. The boundary between ethical and unethical information expectations from recruits is easy to see at the extremes but far more difficult to interpret in the grey, middle ground.

All employers recognise that past employees will use the knowledge and experience they have gained whilst working with them to further their career prospects with a new employer. They expect the employee to recount information about how things are done by their previous employers, the client base and the qualities of their former colleagues. They do not expect, or find it acceptable for, a former employee to take and pass on anything tangible which is not in the public domain such as confidential documents and plans – even those they have compiled themselves. But how do you treat detailed information about impending new product launches, albeit not described in detail or documented? Leaks of such information can be damaging to the past employer but the employee's allegiance is to his new employer and, however desirable it may be, it unrealistic to expect staff to remain completely silent.

In most cases the leakage of information via departing employees has only a transitory effect and is treated as a risk of being in business. Just occasionally it becomes a major issue, and this is usually when the amount of damage is judged to be severe and the methods of passing on information can be shown to be illegal. When Jose Ignacio Lopez left General Motors (GM) in 1993 to join Volkswagen and was followed by a group of his former colleagues, they took enough information with them for General Motors to initiate a legal case against Volkswagen. In 1997 the move succeeded when General Motors obtained a $1.1 billion settlement from Volkswagen. The General Motors legal team claimed that General Motors had been 'victimised by international piracy of their intellectual property rights'. They asserted that General Motors had been subject to unfair competition practices when former executives illegally took boxes of trade secrets with them when they left the company, and used the Racketeer Influenced Corrupt Organisation (RICO) Act to protect GM's intellectual property rights.

A more subtle form of retribution was exacted by Virgin when a former British Airways senior employee joined them but left within weeks, claiming that the job was not what he had been promised. In a letter published in the marketing press Virgin refuted his statement and assured him that the files he had brought over with him from British Airways were being posted back to him!

To maximise the value of internal human intelligence staff need to be encouraged to **collect** it and **report** into the marketing information system on a regular basis. This is more difficult than it sounds. With a few exceptions, notably the salesforce, collecting information is not a natural part of the daily routine of most staff, nor are they necessarily in a position to asses the significance of the information they obtain. Nevertheless, a system for information collection and some type of formal or informal encouragement to report information should be put in place to maximise the information flow. The danger in doing so is that the information flow may be overstimulated and that too much useless or inaccurate information will be reported, potentially resulting in a loss of credibility in the system. This can be avoided by using computerised information collection systems which categorise, filter and validate inputs before permitting them to be disseminated.

Company records and documents

Company records and documents are an equally valuable source of market information (Box 6.2).

To the extent that the company's business reflects the patterns which apply in the market as a whole, internal records will provide an indication of the structure of the marketplace. However, other than in direct selling operations, internal records of the type described will reveal very little about the structure of the customer base.

It is not uncommon for the list of information to be supplemented by additional market and competitor information such as:

● competitors' catalogues
● price lists

- annual reports
- trade association data
- reports on distributors
- reports on customers and potential customers detailing:
  - their **total** demand
  - **products** purchased
  - suppliers used
  - their **service requirements** from suppliers
- import and export statistics.

Apart from major companies that have established marketing information systems, it is rare for internally held data to be brought together into a common database, to be analysed and interpreted to show a market pattern. Those holding internal data often do so for reasons other than market research and may well be oblivious to its usefulness for research purposes. For example difficulties are frequently encountered when seeking a full list of customers. The most common source of a complete and up-to-date list of customers is the accounts department which produces it from invoice records held on the accounting system. Such lists can suffer from the following problems which limit their usefulness for market research purposes:

- the address to which invoices are sent may not be the shipment address for products
- individuals' names on invoices may not be the name of the buyer
- where invoices are originated by different departments, total shipments to individual customers may be difficult to aggregate
- little, if any, data about the customer can be incorporated in the list.

Box 6.2 Company records and documents

Such documents should yield the following information as a minimum:

- **company's own sales by**:
  - product type
  - customer type
  - region
  - by price band
- **average** order sizes
- **range** of order sizes
- order **intervals**
- **seasonal patterns** of sales
- **regular**, **repeat** and **new** customer sales
- **customer databases** (such as guarantee cards, repair records, loyalty scheme membership).

Some of these problems are overcome, at least in part by the newer sources of lists now available. Loyalty cardholders are required to provide information about themselves which extends beyond their name and address, thereby making them more useful for research purposes. Indeed, one of the primary benefits of loyalty schemes is the detailed customer information they provide and the opportunities they create to track purchasing patterns. These opportunities will expand as loyalty card operators switch from magnetic strip cards to 'smart' cards which can hold substantial amounts of data on an electronic chip.

Data on customers can be significantly enhanced by merging the information contained in customer databases with geodemographic databases (see geodemographics in Chapter 8).

6.2 The Accuracy of Internal Information

As a rule internally held data is strong on what the company does itself but weak on the market as a whole. It is also strong on numerical data and weak on qualitative information which leads to an understanding of customer decision making. The accuracy, and therefore the usefulness, of the data from internal sources can be assessed by checking:

- **The time it was obtained** – old information is likely to be less accurate or representative of the current situation than recent information.
- **The method by which it was acquired** – data which has been collected from first-hand sources (e.g. direct from customers) tends to be more reliable than indirect reports.
- **Who acquired the information** – some internal sources are more objective and reliable than others; data collected by sales teams is commonly less accurate than information derived from accounts records
- **The purpose for which the data was acquired** – data may be biased or incomplete because it was obtained to solve a highly specific problem.

6.3 The Information Audit

As a precursor to any activity which might result in commissioning external research, it is useful to carry out an audit of the information which already exists within the organisation. The requirements of knowledge management systems also dictate that such an exercise is completed so that the data and the holders of the data can be incorporated into the system.

6.4 The Information Gap

The data which needs to be obtained by market research techniques is the difference between what is **required** and what is **available** from internal sources. In defining the requirement, account needs to be taken of:

- the feasibility of filling the information gaps by market research techniques
- the levels of accuracy that can be achieved.

There is much information which it is desirable to have but which cannot be obtained ethically or at a cost which would be justified by the use to which it is to be put. The problem exists most commonly with respect to information on competitors' activities. Whilst it may be of considerable advantage to obtain a copy of their strategic plans or new product proposals, these are not legitimate research objectives other than to the extent to which they can be interpolated or inferred from publicly available information.

Problems may also exist with customer data where research users are constantly pushing at the boundaries of what it is ethical for researchers to provide. Many users see research as a preliminary to sales efforts or as a sales prospecting exercise. This leads them to specify information which shows not just what the market as a whole requires but also information on what **individual** customers want or intend to do. If a research programme identifies individuals that are intending to buy or are in the process of buying specific items it is very tempting to use this data to initiate an immediate sales approach. To do so brings research into disrepute and makes legitimate research efforts more difficult to implement in the future.

Accuracy is a perennial problem in research. The accuracy of most data can be controlled through the sampling process and the data collection method, but some topics are inherently difficult to cover and accurate information may prove too difficult to obtain because respondents are either unwilling to answer questions or give a false response. Sensitive topics among individuals include anything to do with sex, personal hygiene and personal finances. Among corporate respondents they may include anything to do with product formulations, production methods and finances. Where the subject matter is such that the accuracy of the findings is in doubt, it is advisable to check that the research approach is likely to overcome the problems and, if not, to abandon the research exercise.

6.5 External Published Information

The information age has been characterised by an ever-growing corpus of published information on companies, industries, products and markets of all types. The sources of information are as diverse as the subjects they

---

Box 6.3 External published information

The depth and quality of information available varies considerably from market sector to market sector and from country to country but a diligent search can be expected to yield data on:

- population size, structure in geodemographic groups and growth
- the structure of distribution and the importance of various channels
- imports and exports by origin and destination
- total sales
- production by product type
- products available and their specifications
- new product launches
- sources of supply
- distribution channels
- list prices
- new contracts and successful bidders for outstanding contracts
- advertising expenditure by product, industry sector and supplier
- new market entrants
- staff movements
- financial performance of suppliers.

---

cover. Secondary (or desk) research is still an undervalued research technique often relegated to the role of providing clues which will verify data collected by primary research techniques. However, if used properly, desk research can make a significant contribution to the basic information required for market analysis (Box 6.3).

The sources of published information are too numerous to list in their entirety and the process of source identification is a skill which takes time to acquire. Researchers are assisted by the existence of a number of 'sources on sources', such as Marketsearch, Findex, Predicasts, the Research Index and Reports Index, which collectively list most of the data that is available, but none of these completely replace experience and persistence as the means of identifying everything relevant that is available. The checklist (Box 6.4) shows the diversity of secondary sources that are available and provides an indication of where to commence a search.

Much published information is available free of charge or at very low cost. The main disadvantage is that sources can be highly fragmented and the data collection process can be time-consuming. There is, however, an increasing trend to publish research reports on specific products, industries or activities which bring together the data available from secondary sources and are designed to provide researchers with comprehensive overviews of markets. These reports, commonly available at relatively low cost, provide the useful function of pre-digesting and harmonising information and sometimes add an element of primary research to support the data obtained from secondary sources.

Box 6.4 Key secondary sources of market information

Government and other official sources

Statistical departments of national governments

Government departments

Company registration/filing organisations

International organisations

Trading and trade promotion organisations

Embassies and consulates

Regional development organisations

Courts

Government research laboratories

Patent offices

Industrial and commercial associations

Trade associations

Industry technical research institutes

Trade federations

Chambers of commerce

Directories

Trade directories

Buyers guides

Exhibition and trade show guides

Catalogues

Telephone white pages

Yellow pages

Company histories

Mail order catalogues

University career guides

Educational and research organisations

Business schools

Universities

Research units of political parties

Trade unions

Publications

Financial press

Daily and weekly press

Regional and local newspapers

Periodicals

Technical and professional journals

Trade press

Industry newsletters

Market research publishers

Financial institutions

National banks

International development banks

Stock exchanges

Stockbroker analysts

Credit report publishers

Companies

Annual reports and accounts

Prospectuses

Product brochures

Technical data sheets

Published technical papers

Marketing materials

Press releases

Advertisements

Seminar handouts

Planning applications

Company magazines

Company newsletters

6.6 **Where to Find Secondary Information – Manual Searches**

The most accessible sources of secondary information are public, educational and specialist libraries. A well stocked library represents a major asset to any business community and there are many which facilitate the secondary research process by amassing a wide range of major and minor sources. The types of library to approach are:

- Central reference libraries
- Major municipal libraries
- University libraries
- Business school libraries
- Government department libraries
- Research establishment libraries
- Company libraries
- The libraries of professional bodies.

There are in addition a host of specialist libraries dealing with individual subjects or particular geographical regions. Access to libraries, particularly those set up for the use of an organisation's members, staff or students, may prove to be a problem but the library community tends to be one in which there is considerable sharing of resources. It is therefore possible that a

---

Box 6.5 Database search information

The key types of information which can be collected more efficiently by a database search are:

- Local, national and international news items
- Trade press items
- Business and professional journals
- Company financial information
- Information on mergers and acquisitions
- Government information
- Economic data
- Patents
- Citations
- Trademarks
- Scientific and technical information
- Medical and healthcare literature
- Legal information
- Tax information
- Information on currency
- Share prices
- Biographies of businessmen and businesswomen.

---

source not held in a local reference library can be obtained on loan by the librarian from a library which does stock it. Special visitor permits to use a library which is normally closed to outsiders may be available on request or for the payment of a small fee.

6.7 Electronic Searches

There is a growing trend to collect data into computerised databases which are available either online or on CD Roms for efficient and rapid searching. Host organisations running online services have a strong financial incentive to expand the range of information they carry and suppliers of information are equally interested in expanding their customer base by facilitating the acquisition of what they have to offer. Many of the secondary sources identified above are available online either on specialist business databases or the Internet.

Although some market research companies, such as Nielsen, Freedonia and Frost and Sullivan, distribute their syndicated information online, most databases have a strong orientation towards particular types of information which limits their usefulness for general market research.

Many of the sources on sources listed above, such as Findex, and magazine indexes are available online which offers the potential to identify useful studies and articles efficiently even if the documents themselves have to be obtained in hard copy.

The number of databases available online is expanding quickly as improvements in technology facilitate their use and as customer pressure for more information creates additional markets.

6.8 The Internet

The internet is a rapidly growing method of accessing secondary information from world-wide sources and as more organisations are connected it is set to displace a high proportion of physical searches in libraries. The use of the internet as a research tool is discussed in detail in Chapter 12.

Sampling

The most accurate method of quantifying a market would be to carry out a census of all the individuals or organisations who are active within it. However, apart from some industrial markets in which the number of purchasers is very small, a census is rarely practical. Nor, in the past, have they been economic though the ever-widening use of electronic point of sale (EPOS) equipment has facilitated the collection of purchase data from censuses of retail customers. Fortunately, in the post-war period statistical methods have advanced to the point where samples of the participants in any market can provide data which, though not completely accurate, is sufficiently accurate for marketing decision making.

A sample is a part of the universe which, if studied, **can be used to draw conclusions about the universe as a whole**. Sampling is the process which ensures that the sample adequately represents the universe from which it is taken. All samples are subject to 'sample error' but the extent of the error can be adjusted by varying the sample size. As samples become larger the accuracy of the results increases. Statistical analysis can be used to quantify the probability of the error in results computed from a samples of varying sizes and structures. This means that there can be a low-, medium- and high-cost answer to any question and that survey accuracy can be modulated to take account of external factors, such as the applications for the data and the budget available. The difference between the different approaches is not the data but the level of confidence that can be placed in results.

Sampling is an integral part of survey research but is a subject of such tediousness and complexity that most research users have a mental blockage when it comes to understanding it. This can apply to research practitioners as well, many of whom are only too happy to delegate responsibility for sampling to their statisticians and field managers. Many of the problems which research users have with sampling arise from the use of terminology which is unfamiliar. These relate primarily to the statistical techniques for estimating the size of sample to be employed and for testing the validity/ accuracy of the results. Most of these terms are defined in any basic statistical textbook and will not be repeated here, but in any case commercial survey work tends to be carried out on a highly pragmatic basis, to a budget and within a time frame which precludes complex and expensive sampling procedures.

7.1 The Theory of Sampling

The use of a sample survey to measure markets requires that the sample be **statistically representative**, and structured to reflect the various types of individuals or units that make up the universe of customers. To achieve this requires either that the sample is drawn in such a way that it automatically represents the universe or that the structure is known in advance and quotas are set for component segments of the universe. As we will show later, it is also possible to draw a sample which **reflects** (rather than represents) the segments of a customer base and to adjust the results retrospectively to bring them into line with the structure of market. With the exception of **random** sampling, all techniques require some knowledge of the marketplace other than that derived from the sample itself in order to ensure that the results are accurate.

7.2 Key Issues in Sampling

Although statistical theory can be complex, the key issues which determine the accuracy and usefulness of a survey are not. In summary they are:

- the **size and structure** of the universe to be sampled
- the identity of the **respondents** to be sampled (the sampling unit)
- the **size** of sample to employed
- the **source** of sample names
- the **sampling procedure** to be adopted

The universe to be sampled

Before any consideration can be given to the size and type of sample to be drawn it is essential to define the **size and structure of the universe from which the sample will be drawn**. The definition will depend entirely on the product or service being researched and the characteristics of those purchasing or using it. In surveys where wide segments of the population are qualified to answer questions, the definition of the universe is relatively straightforward. Products which are widely and frequently purchased (such as personal hygiene items) require samples drawn from broad segments of the population, such as all adults, males or females in certain age groups, and in such cases the universe is easy to define. As the products or services become more specialised the universe becomes progressively more difficult to define. Research exercises covering those who have fax machines or modems installed in their homes or who use personal accountancy services will encounter many more difficulties in defining the universe, and in some cases it may prove impossible to obtain reliable data other than by a random sample approach.

The most common parameters for universe definition in the three key areas of research are:

Consumer research
- Age
- Sex
- Marital status
- Family structure
- Income level
- Location of residence
- Ownership of specific items
- Recent purchases of specific items.

Trade research
- Type and size of store
- Products stocked
- Store location.

Industrial research
- Industry sector
- Size of company
- Geographical location.

In some situations, it is also possible to quantify the various **components of the universe**. Demographic information will normally provide the numbers of males and females in particular age groups or resident in specific geographical areas sufficiently accurately to show the overall structure of the universe. Information on the numbers that have purchased specific products is less likely to be available. Business censuses and surveys will commonly show the number of companies active in each industrial and commercial sector and each geographical region sufficiently accurately to profile the universe.

Sampling unit

The type of respondent to be sampled in a research exercise is determined largely by the information that is to be collected and the characteristics of the purchaser or the purchasing unit. Clearly responses are required from those who are qualified to provide the data required. These are normally key decision makers, defined by the fact that they purchase the products or services concerned, or are individuals in a position to influence purchase decisions. Depending on the product or service to be covered and the nature of the research it may be necessary to cover **all classes of purchaser** (defined by age, sex, income group, geographical region or activity) or only **specific segments** of the market (e.g. males in specific age groups). The most common groups of respondents in market research are.

Consumer research
- Individuals (men, women, children classified by age, income group or situation – e.g. heads of households or mothers with young children, ownership of specific products and areas of residence).

Trade research
- Retail outlets
- Wholesalers
- Specialist distribution channels (e.g. computer value-added resellers).

Industrial research
- Buyers, specifiers and users of finished products and services within user companies
- Intermediaries purchasing components to assemble finished products
- Trade wholesalers and factors
- Suppliers of raw materials
- Specifiers (e.g. architects and consultants)
- Advisors
- Designers
- Competitors.

Sample size

The prime determinants of the size of sample required are the homogeneity of the universe and the level of detail and accuracy required in the final analysis (Box 7.1). Samples of several thousand, structured by income group, lifestyle or region are regularly used to represent national populations of tens of millions but if the analysis is required by fine breakdowns of customer type the numbers can increase dramatically. Sample numbers are also affected by the characteristic of the product being surveyed. Products or services purchased frequently by a high proportion of individuals, such as food and drink, can be researched using relatively small samples. Products or services purchased infrequently, such as automobiles or consumer durables, may require large samples simply to identify customers that have made a purchase within the recent past.

Where statistical samples are used, the size of the sample is determined by the **margin of error** that is permissible and the **level of confidence** that must not be exceeded in the results. Broadly, the size of the sample increases as the permitted margin of error reduces and the level of confidence increases. The one aspect of a marketplace which does *not* normally contribute to the determination of the size of the sample is the number of customers. For any given level of accuracy, markets with large numbers of customers require the same size of sample as markets which have only small numbers of customers.

Box 7.1 Sample sizes

Sample sizes are generally determined by a variety of techniques not all of which have much to do with statistical theory. These include:

- **Judgement** – the size of sample that feels right and will be judged by management as being capable of delivering accurate results. Such samples often end up being larger than necessary because management finds it difficult to accept that small numbers will produce accurate results.
- **Budget** – the maximum number of interviews that the budget for the survey will permit. Although highly pragmatic, this approach may require compromises on accuracy if sample sizes prove inadequate.
- **Statistical methods** – the use of statistical theory to determine the size of sample that will yield results within a quantifiable statistical error.

Box 7.2 shows the random samples that are required to achieve various combinations of statistical margins of error and levels of confidence.

It is evident from the data in Box 7.2 that the size of the sample escalates rapidly as accuracy and confidence limits increase. Furthermore, the numbers apply to margins of error and levels of confidence across the sample as a whole. If an analysis based on sub-sets of the sample is required then the sample numbers need to be achieved for each sub-set.

High levels of statistical accuracy therefore impose a considerable cost burden on those commissioning surveys and it is often essential to take a

---

Box 7.2 Sample sizes for given levels of statistical error

Margin of error (+ or –) (%)	Level of confidence (%)							
	50	75	80	85	90	95	99	99.9
1.0	1,140	3,307	4,096	5,184	6,766	9,604	16,590	19,741
2.0	285	827	1,024	1,296	1,692	2,401	4,148	4,936
3.0	127	358	456	576	752	1,068	1,844	2,194
4.0	72	207	256	324	423	601	1,037	1,234
5.0	46	133	164	208	271	385	664	790
7.5	21	59	73	93	121	171	296	351
10.0	12	34	41	52	68	97	166	198
15.0	6	15	19	24	31	43	74	88
20.0	3	9	11	13	17	25	42	50
50.0	2	2	2	3	3	4	7	10

pragmatic approach which identifies the levels of accuracy which are **good enough** for the decision being taken, rather than always seeking the best data.

Source of sample

Samples can be sourced in a variety of ways which can broadly be categorised as:

- 'on-the-ground' sampling
- sampling from predefined lists and 'random walks' of names
- use of organisations that specialise in the provision of samples.

On-the-ground sampling is common in consumer research where suitable respondents can be identified either by stopping them at random in shopping precincts, stopping them at locations which have an affinity with the subject being studied (e.g. travellers at airports) or by calling at their homes (the location and type of house often being used as an indication of suitability).

'Random walks' are a mechanism for randomly selecting households within defined geographical areas. They are implemented through a set of random instructions which direct interviewers from a given starting point to the households to be interviewed.

The use of **lists** as sources of samples is an ideal approach, provided they contain all of the units that qualify for the research. Unfortunately, comprehensive and up-to-date lists are rarely available outside highly specific situations – such as lists of all government departments or companies quoted on stock exchanges. Lists of consumers rely on official sources such as electoral registers or (in some countries) tax payers (Box 7.3). Although these lists are updated regularly, population movement soon introduces a significant proportion of inaccurate listings. Residential telephone directories offer an alternative source of consumer names but are subject to a number of fundamental problems which limit their usefulness for research. First, they too fail to keep pace with population mobility. Second, they exclude the growing number of home owners who choose not to have their numbers listed.[1] Third, they are unlikely to keep pace with frequent changes in dialling codes which are made when systems are adapted to cope with rapid expansion in the demand for telephone lines. Finally, telephone lists contain a number of biases. Certain groups within the population, such as the elderly, lower income groups, ethnic minorities, street traders and salespeople,[2] are less likely to own or be accessible by a telephone. Furthermore, the characteristics of households which are unlisted in directories, either inadvertently or deliberately, can differ from those which are listed. Those which are highly mobile may never stay still long enough to get listed and those who chose to be ex-directory may be in above-average income groups or in specific occupations.

Box 7.3 Sources of lists used in market research

The major sources of lists that are used in market research include:

- electoral registers
- geodemographic databases[3]
- residential telephone directories
- *Yellow Pages*
- business directories
- subscriber lists for magazines and journals
- membership lists for organisations.

For business research, *Yellow Pages*, which identify the activity and location of companies, are a good starting point, but more refined listings which show the sizes of companies, details of their product ranges and services and key personnel are rarely accurate enough for a highly scientific sampling approach without further work being done on them. The quality of business lists varies considerably from country to country. North European and North American countries are generally well serviced with lists which are sufficiently accurate to act as a starting point for research. In faster-moving economies, such as those of South East Asia, such lists as are available become outdated very quickly. In the less developed world lists of any type are rare.

Organisations that specialise in the provision of sample information for market research purposes overcome some of the problems associated with the lists described above. Their most valuable contribution is to **clean lists** to ensure that the addresses and telephone numbers are valid. They can also balance samples geographically to ensure that they are geographically representative. Such organisations are specialists in either lifestyle or geodemographic research,[4] for which the sale of sample data is an incremental source of income, or organisations whose mainstream business is the sale of samples for research purposes. The use of list brokers whose function is to source lists of particular categories of individuals or companies is an option but not a highly attractive one. The sources that they use, such as magazine subscription lists, are rarely comprehensive or up-to-date and may contain significant biases. However, as a source of last resort, when all other methods of identifying suitable respondents have failed, they are certainly better than nothing.

Sampling procedure

Sampling is an exact science but in market research it is usually practised pragmatically. The true random (or probability) sample, in which all units of the universe have an equal chance of appearing in the sample, is rarely used – mainly because it is too costly to implement. The most common approach is the **quota sample**, in which quotas are set for respondents fulfilling certain criteria. Individuals are then screened to determine whether they fit one of the quotas and interviewing proceeds until the quotas are filled.

Geographically random samples are feasible using telephone interviews but are commonly abandoned in favour of random locations, which concentrate interviewing in specific parts of the territory.

Random digit dialling is a procedure used in telephone surveys to side-step the problems associated with lists and sample selection. Computer-generated lists of random (and feasible) telephone numbers coupled with screening questions to categorise those that respond provide a method of identifying truly random samples of consumers or business establishments. Unless procedures are in place to remove unwanted numbers – such as business numbers from consumer samples and vice versa – there is obviously a significant number of wasted calls, but the cost of these can be lower than other methods of sample generation.

One word of warning: the use of random digit dialling requires that interviewers are briefed to answer questions about how the number was obtained whenever ex-directory numbers are dialled. Access by strangers to such numbers is likely to cause hostility and a high refusal rate.

7.3 **Sample error**

Error arises in samples when they fail to adequately represent all categories of customer. They can occur for a number of reasons. The most common are a bias towards particular types of customer, the exclusion of important customer groups and non-response.

Bias can occur as a consequence of the way in which the sample is **structured** or the way in which it is **selected**, either of which can favour particular individuals or groups of customers. Structuring problems arise when there is insufficient knowledge about a market to ensure that all customer types are adequately represented. This can happen in the case of new products and products which have a significant customer base outside that being targeted by manufacturers. Selection problems can arise out of inadequate interviewer briefing or an incorrect application of sampling instructions.

For example, even when working within strict quotas, street interviewers will tend to select those who look friendly rather than those appear hostile and those who look as though they will understand the questions rather than those who seem likely to cause problems. When approaching residences they may avoid those which look dilapidated, those at the top of tower blocks and those which are home to large and apparently vicious dogs. This can result in the young, the old and the apparently infirm being excluded from the sample. The over-representation of some groups of the population and the under-representation of others will lead to results which do not represent the population as a whole. The sample design strategy must seek to eliminate or at least minimise these problems.

Exclusion of important customer groups will have the same effect since their activities or opinions will not be included in the overall analysis. The seriousness of the consequent distortion will depend on the extent to which the activities of the groups or individuals which are excluded differ from those of the sampled population.

Non-response is the element of a sample that refuses to reply to questionnaires – or having been selected, cannot be contacted. Errors arising from non-response distort survey results if reluctance to respond is associated with particular types of customer, thereby creating the same type of problem as bias and exclusion.

The level of sample error can be reduced either by increasing the size of the sample or by improving the amount of knowledge on the structure of the market prior to drawing the sample. Large samples have a lower risk of bias than small samples and are also more likely to include all types of customers.

7.4 **Descriptive and Inferential Statistics**

The results of sample surveys are used both **descriptively** and **inferentially**. The former describes the practices, attitudes or requirements of those that have been sampled. The latter uses the results of the sample survey to describe what is happening in the population as a whole. If the sample is itself representative of the universe being studied, a description of the sample can be used without adjustment to infer what is happening in the universe as a whole. If the sample has been structured so that it reflects different segments of the market a weighting exercise will be required in order to obtain results which show what is happening in the universe.

For example, a shop that wishes to describe the requirements of its customers can do so as follows. It divides its overall customer base into homogeneous categories – say, by sex and by age group. It then interviews a sample of each customer category in order to determine what they require. The results could differ quite significantly by customer group, as shown in Box 7.4.

Box 7.4 describes the requirements of each market segment to the accuracy limits set by the sample size. However, the arithmetic average of the total sample describes the requirements of the shop's customer base only if the segments used for the sample are of equal importance in the shop's **actual customer base**. The probability is that they are not, in which case further customer analysis is required to show the division of the customer

Box 7.4 Results by customer

Group		% of sample requiring			
	Base	24-hour opening	Provision of cash dispensers	On-site car parking	Petrol forecourt
Women					
15–25	300	15	75	25	30
26–40	300	10	80	85	80
Over 40	300	5	82	70	65
Men					
15–25	300	25	65	35	30
26–40	300	50	60	65	60
Over 40	300	20	45	50	55
Total	1,800	39	68	55	53

base by sex and by age group. The results of this analysis can then be used to compute the requirements of the customer base as a whole, as shown in Box 7.5. In this example the shop has a customer base dominated by younger women, and their requirements should therefore have a greater influence on the services provided. The weighted totals show the effect of their added influence on overall customer requirements.

7.5 Sampling in industrial markets

The structure of many industrial markets precludes sampling of the type described above. Some industrial markets contain so few buyers that a census is not only practical but essential to say anything meaningful about customers. Others are large enough for sampling but are too complex for simple sampling procedures.

Sample stratification

Industrial sampling requires careful stratification of the market in order to ensure representativeness. This is no different in principle from consumer research only more complex to apply. Unless they have carried out research before, most manufacturers have only a rudimentary knowledge of the structure of the market in which they are operating and any guidance they give must be treated with caution. Secondary sources may be of some help but these, too, can prove to be inadequate.

Box 7.5 Customer base

	Sample base	Weights	% of sample requiring			
			24-hour opening	Provision of cash dispensers	On-site car parking	Petrol forecourt
Women						
15–25	300	30	15	75	25	30
26–40	300	35	10	80	85	80
Over 40	300	12	5	82	70	65
Men						
15–25	300	5	25	65	35	30
26–40	300	13	50	60	65	60
Over 40	300	5	20	45	50	55
Total	1,800	100	21	68	55	53
Weighted total			17	74	58	57

Universe definition

Even if the structure of the market is known, it is not often that the universe can be defined accurately. Whereas the size and structure of consumer markets can be estimated from census data and from regular surveys, industrial markets are rarely quantified to the same level of refinement. This is mainly due to the complexity of industrial markets and the large number of specialisations which can exist within them. Knowing that a company manufactures chemicals is completely inadequate if the sample needs to cover only those manufacturing a particular type of flame retardant. Although statistics are compiled showing the total number of companies in each industrial sector, the sector classifications tend to be extremely broad and there is rarely adequate information on each of the detailed specialist activities within sectors.

This normally means that the **definition of the universe** is an integral and important part of the research process itself and must be carried out before any sampling exercises can begin. It will rely on a combination of secondary sources, data obtained from the client company and interviews with individuals or organisations who may have information on who is active within particular industry sectors. Trade associations can be an important part of this process, though not all of them are prepared to reveal their membership.

Pareto's Law

The saving factor in many industrial markets is Pareto's Law (or the 80/20 rule). Unfortunately it is also a major potential source of sampling problems. Pareto's Law states that 80 per cent of demand is derived from 20 per cent of customers. This permits an industrial sample to cover a high proportion of demand by including all major buyers and sampling the remainder of the customer base. To apply this rule means that the major customers must be identifiable – a process which may be straightforward but may also rely heavily on information from suppliers and distributors. The most significant problem which can arise is that if one of the major customers is excluded from the survey, a significant proportion of demand is also excluded.

Notes

1 An estimated 34 per cent of UK households are ex-directory.
2 Mobile telephone ownership among some groups may overcome this problem, but the mobile telephone is far from ideal as a medium for survey research.
3 See Chapter 8.
4 Such as CACI (Acorn), CCN (Mosaic), CDMS (Super Profiles), Infolink (Define) and Equifax (Images).

8 Target Marketing and Market Classification Systems

In order to market more effectively there is a growing need for suppliers to tailor their product and service offers not to the marketplace as a whole but to those segments of the market that they have identified, for whatever reason, as being particularly attractive to them. One of the most important changes that has occurred in markets in the last 20 years has been the replacement of the 'herd instinct' by a need for individual expression. This is being achieved in part through purchasing and consumption patterns and has resulted in a **fragmentation of markets** into segments of ever-reducing size. In response, segmented, or target marketing has gradually replaced mass marketing as the standard method of structuring a marketing plan.

Target marketing is attractive to suppliers because it makes the marketing task easier, increases the opportunities for differentiation and improves marketing efficiency. Marketing to small, homogeneous groups of customers is considerably more straightforward than mass-marketing campaigns designed to reach large, disparate audiences. The marketing messages work better because suppliers are more likely to be saying what customers want to hear and the channels of communication are simpler. Working within a segment, suppliers also have greater opportunity to differentiate themselves and, by developing a closer affinity with customers, reduce the impact of competition. In essence the advantages are those of being 'a big fish in a little pond rather than a little fish in a big pond' which, provided the pond is big enough to satisfy ambitions, can be a more comfortable and secure lifestyle.

The growth of target marketing has been facilitated by the introduction of manufacturing systems which permit the production of small volumes of customised products designed to meet the needs of specialist groups of customers at acceptable cost levels. Whereas the need for mass marketing was created by the advantages of mass production, target marketing has been made feasible by flexible manufacturing systems. This has been accompanied the refinement of communication media so that it is increasingly possible to address individual segments of markets.

Key requirements for target marketing are that the requirements of customers in each segment of the market are clearly differentiated from those in other segments and that customers are responsive to the messages directed at them. There must also be unique channels of communication to the segments. If these criteria are not met, there is no advantage to be gained from attempting to target segments separately. There must also be a basis for **classifying the segments**. This can be done according to a number of criteria of which the some of the most important are:

- geography (country, region or city)
- demographics (age, sex, occupation, income, race, religion)
- social class
- psychographic variables such as lifestyle, attitudes and personality traits
- benefits sought
- purchase volumes (light, medium or heavy buyers)
- purchase frequency (regular, intermittent or infreqent buyers)
- mindset (such as, novice or experienced buyer).

In industrial marketing the need for a targeted approach is even more important since industrial markets tend to be more heavily segmented than consumer markets and there are likely to be more significant differences between the requirements of individual customers. Industry segmentation is typically based on:

- location
- company size
- ownership
- industry sector
- manufacturing technology
- benefits sought.

Research plays a front-line role in the development of a target marketing strategy by determining whether separate segments exist within a market, the criteria which can be used to define them and the specific requirements of each segment. Research achieves this either by analysing according to predetermined market classifications or by retrospecively examining the data that has been collected to determine whether there is a clustering of product or service requirements around particular customer characteristics.

Classification data which can be used to identify segments, describe their characteristics and locate respondents within them in advance of the research can come from a variety of sources including:

- the national Census
- geodemographic databases (which are based on Census data)
- consumer panel data
- customer records held by companies (such as guarantee registration cards and loyalty scheme members).

While each of these is of considerable value, is improving and is used extensively for segmentation research, a high proportion of survey work still relies on **retrospective classifications** using data collected in the course of the survey.

8.1 Socio-economic classifications (Box 8.1)

The segmentation criteria for consumers outlined above can all be applied in a research exercise but are generally too complex to be used in their entirety unless there is reason for suspecting that they are relevant. For example, an ethnic marketing strategy for any product in which consumers' origins could determine product or service requirements would use ethnic origin as a key segmenatation criterion, but for most analyses the segmentation criteria have tended to be simplified.

The socio-economic system has the advantage of being relatively easy to apply compared with more refined criteria, especially in an interview situation. It is nevertheless a crude classification and has become outdated.

Box 8.1 The socio-economic group

The tried and tested method of classifying customers is the **socio-economic group** which combines social class and occupation of the head of the household in order to describe the key groupings of customers. They are as follows:

A	Upper middle class	Higher managerial, administrative and professional
B	Middle class	Intermediate managerial, administrative or professional
C1	Lower middle class	Supervisory or clerical and junior managerial, administrative or professional
C2	Skilled working class	Skilled manual workers
D	Working class	Semi-skilled and unskilled manual workers
E	Those at the lowest levels of subsistence	State pensioners or widows (no other earner), casual or lowest grade workers

---

8.2 Geodemographics

The ultimate in research is a database which contains descriptive information on all consumers – such as their sex, age, marital status, income levels, assets, ownership of various products, readership and leisure practices – plus a record of all their new purchases showing brands, source of purchase, prices paid and payment methods. Such a database would provide an instant response to most questions relating to the size and structure of markets, disribution and the success or otherwise of new products and promotional programnmes.

Geodemographic databases represent a small step in this direction. By combining demographic information, initially drawn from the national

Census, with a geographical database, initially the Census Enumeration Districts, geodemograpics provides **a national classification of small areas according to the characteristics of their inhabitants**. A Census Enumeration District comprises approximately 150 households – a long way from individual consumers but a lot more refined than any previous classification system.

The earliest known geodemographic map was that produced by Charles Booth for his *Life and Labour of the People of London*, in 1889. To create it, Booth carried out a census of London neighbourhoods and classified them into eight groups. These were:

- **lowest class** – vicious semi-criminals
- **very poor**
- **mixed** – some comfortable, others poor
- **fairly comfortable** – good ordinary earnings
- **well-to-do** – middle class
- **upper-middle** and **upper class** – wealthy.

The research demonstrated for the first time that neighbourhoods could display common population characteristics

Since its inception in the 1970s the use of geodemographic databases has expanded rapidly as a growing number of applications have been developed. Market research has been an important beneficiary.

Knowledge of the structure of the consumer universe, and therefore the types of sample that need to be drawn, has been considerably enhanced by the development of geodemographic and life style information. The segmentation of consumers by socio-economic group, implied that the requirements and expenditure patterns of high-income, managerial grades and other key groups were reasonably homogeneous. This system worked reasonably well for years even though the category into which a respondent fell could not normally be determined until they were interviewed.

It was then shown that the **type of residence and its location**, as defined by postcode, was not only a more effective predictor of purchases but was also more accessible. Thus geodemographic groups have become increasingly widely used as sample criteria. Similarly, life style research has shown that definitions such as age, marital status and size of family can be replaced by descriptors which take account of the aspirations and perceptions of individual consumers. 'Yuppies' and 'empty-nesters' have distinct expenditure patterns which are unique to them and enable suppliers to apply a more relevant segmentation approach to their marketing.

8.3 Industrial classifications

The classification of industrial markets has traditionally been more straightforward than consumer markets. It has relied on activity classifications, as embodied in the various Standard Industrial Classifications (SICs), which group companies according to the products they manufacture or the services they provide. However, industrial markets have become increasingly sophisticated and activity classifications have become less satisfactory as a means of categorising companies. Whilst it is certainly true that companies in the steel, chemical or machine tools industries share common requirements in terms of the raw materials and components they purchase, the criteria which determine their purchases of telecommunications, office equipment, stationery or vehicles are more likely to be related to their size, workforce characteristics, age, experience, ownership or location.

There has also been a growing emphasis on segmentations based on the **benefits sought by industrial buyers from their suppliers**. Depending on how they are positioning themselves with their own customer base, industrial buyers can place differing emphases on supply factors such as product performance, quality, product consistency, cost, reliability, speed of delivery or technical support. Different combinations of service requirements can define segments just as clearly as activity classifications and, provided they are recognised, can provide a more powerful basis for a segmentation strategy.

The ability to research and recognise the benefit requirements of industrial buyers is hampered only by the fact that the decision making unit is more complex than that which applies in households. Industrial purchasing decisions may be coordinated by a single employee but generally take into account the opinions and requirements of a number of others, some of whom may be identifiable and some who may not. The role of the plant manager, the warehouse manager and the financial director may be evident in decisions relating to purchases of fork lift trucks but the role of the truck operators may not even be acknowledged, even though they can have a strong, 'behind-the-scenes' influence. To make matters worse, the clusters of benefits sought by management are likely to differ considerably from those sought by operators. Management is (rightly) interested in performance and cost factors such as load-carrying capability, speed, fuel economy and purchase price. Operators may be more interested in comfort and safety. Identifying these requirements demands a complex research approach which provides separate analyses for each different group of decision maker.

9 Questionnaires

The questionnaire, however applied, is the general workhorse of all market research activity. The use of a questionnaire ensures that the research is carried out consistently and that the results are collected in a format which facilitates analysis. The format of the questionnaire to be used depends on the type of data to be collected, the number of interviews to be completed and the method of analysis. Large quantitative surveys generally deploy short, highly structured questionnaires which are suitable for machine analysis; qualitative surveys are normally based on small numbers of interviews using a long, unstructured questionnaire which is likely to be analysed by hand. It may also be desirable to use a semi-structured questionnaire which contains both structured and unstructured questions, the former to measure what is known, the latter to capture information which cannot be structured in advance.

In the past, structuring the questionnaire was essential in large-scale surveys. The analysis of open-ended questions relied either on transcription and synthesis or on the assignment of codes retrospectively. Whilst this is achievable with tens of questionnaires it is a daunting and expensive task when the samples rise into the thousands. Postcoding can also prove inaccurate since it relies on the ability of the coder to assign consistent codes to respondent statements. However, structuring gives rise to its own problems. Firstly, it straightjackets the research into the precodes that are determined during the design stage of the questionnaire. It therefore demands considerable advance knowledge in order to ensure that the precodes are correct and complete. It is wasteful and unenlightening to design a questionnaire with multiple options only to find that a high proportion of respondents opt for the 'others' category.

Secondly, structuring can make the format of a questionnaire unacceptably complex. It is far simpler to ask a question such as 'What illnesses have you suffered from in the last five years?' and write in the responses, which will normally be few in number, than to list every conceivable illness the respondent could have suffered from. The third problem with fully structured questionnaires is that they eliminate the spontaneous responses which can both illuminate the market situation and explain the relationships that are located. This is particularly true for industrial and commercial surveys where buying patterns and motivations are rarely simple. Fortunately the introduction of scanning and software, such as SPSS's TextSmart®, which permits the rapid coding and analysis of textual responses to open-ended questions, has opened up the possibility of using open-ended questions on large-scale surveys.

9.1 **Designing the Questionnaire**

The six main stages in designing a questionnaire are:

- **defining the questions** to be asked
- determining the **structure** of the questionnaire
- **forming the questions**
- **assembling** the questionnaire
- **piloting** the questionnaire
- **approving** the questionnaire.

Defining the questions to be asked

The questions to be included on the questionnaire are normally dictated by the research brief. Clearly the questions asked must address the problems which the survey is designed to solve. The ease or difficulty of converting a brief into a questionnaire depends on how well the brief has been thought through. Vague briefs which state the research objectives in very general terms require considerable translation work. Detailed briefs, sometimes including specific questions, make the task considerably easier. Nevertheless, whether it is at the brief-writing stage or at the time the questionnaire is being designed, the research problem has to be converted into a set of questions which provide the research-based solution.

Determining the structure of the questionnaire

Typically the design of a questionnaire takes place in stages. The first stage sets out the **generic objectives** of the questionnaire. In a survey designed to test the effectiveness of a supplier's customer service strategy these could be:

- Are we providing the services our clients require?
- How well do we meet the service objectives of our clients?
- Do we do better or worse than our competitors?
- What do we need to do to improve our performance?

The second stage involves a programme of **exploratory research** which is designed to provide the information on which a detailed questionnaire can be based. The exploratory research should be undertaken in two stages – **internally** with the company's own staff and **externally** with customers. The amount of external exploratory research that is required depends on the amount of information that is likely to be available within the company. Even though a company that has been active in a market for a considerable period of time and has previously studied its customer base will be in a much stronger position to provide guidance than a relative newcomer, it is always advisable to collect information from those of the internal staff that have had client contact before launching an external exploratory research programme. Internal research of this type serves two functions. First it proves data and secondly it shows the perceptions which exist among company staff. In the event that the staff perceptions are out of line with reality, internal analysis provides a basis for any re-education programme which may be required once the survey is completed.

Exploratory research uses a checklist of topics designed to probe those aspects of customer behaviour or attitudes which would be quantified in the full survey. For example, in order to quantify service requirements it is essential to identify all of the aspects of service customers could conceivably require. In order to rate performance against competitors it is necessary to know who is active in the market. Depending on the nature of the problem the exploratory research can be carried out by means of focus groups, in-depth personal interviews or, in a simple case, telephone interviews.

The final stage of the design process converts the generic objectives into a set of specific questions using the results of the exploratory research. It may also elaborate the line of questioning to include related topics which the exploratory research has identified as being important. The biggest danger at this stage arises from the temptation to include extra questions to which it might be nice to know the answers but which are not strictly relevant to the project. This temptation must be avoided since it elongates the questionnaire and prolongs the research unnecessarily.

Forming the questions

One of the key skills in market research is the creation of a questionnaire which is interesting to respondents, elicits the information that is required comprehensively and consistently and in which the questions are unambiguous. For this reason questionnaires tend to rely on simple wording and, wherever possible, check boxes and numerical scales. The need for simplicity is dictated by the fact that in an interview situation there are two people involved, either of which can distort the findings – the respondent by not comprehending the question or by being too bored to concentrate and the interviewer by misrepresenting the question or failing to record the response correctly. Some of these problems can be minimised by using a CATI, CAPI or CASI approach (see Chapter 11) which provides an instant check of the responses and a rejection of replies which are either impossible or inconsistent with previous responses, but the use of computers also demands simple question formats.

Types of questions
Questionnaires generally incorporate one or more of the following types of question (Box 9.1).

Dichotomous questions permit only two responses, commonly 'yes' or 'no' but also variants such as 'agree' or 'disagree' and 'saw' or 'did not see'. The question may also include a supplementary category of response such as

---

Box 9.1 Typical questionnaire questions

● **Closed questions**
  − dichotomous questions
  − multiple-choice questions
  − semantic scales
  − scaling questions
● **Open-ended responses**.

'don't know' or 'no opinion', to cope with lack of knowledge or uncertainty. These questions deal well with clear-cut, factual situations. Their major disadvantage is that they may force a simple response where in reality the situation is more complicated and the reply needs to be caveated – i.e. 'yes but'.

Multiple-choice questions are an extension of the dichotomous approach which offer a list of alternative responses such as a range of brands, a number of alternative retail outlets or a list of criteria which could be considered in the decision to purchase. Multiple selections (e.g. more than one brand purchased) may be permitted, depending on the purpose of the research. Multiple-choice questions are generally simple to complete and to analyse but to be effective all of the options must be included. An excessive response to an 'others' category will dilute the usefulness of the results, unless the 'others' are also named. Furthermore, considerable care has to be taken in the definition of the options. Choosing between brands purchased is relatively straightforward but the selection of more qualitative options such as purchase criteria can easily be biased towards those which the respondent feels *should* be important rather than those which are genuinely taken into account.

Semantic scales are a version of multiple-choice questions which measure customer reaction to propositions by selecting a statement which corresponds most closely to their opinion (Box 9.2). Semantic scales suffer only from the consistency of interpretation of the words used. Whilst there is every chance that respondents will interpret 'honest' and 'dishonest' in a similar way, 'frequency' can too easily mean different things to different respondents.

Scaling question or rating scales measure effectiveness or performance. Although they may use a range of assessments which include 'excellent', 'very good', 'good', 'fair' and 'poor', they commonly seek to overcome problems of interpretation by converting the scales to numerical values in which, for example, 1 equals poor and 10 equals excellent.

Open-ended responses are the staple of qualitative research. They comprise a question, such as 'what do you think of . . .?' and permit any response the respondents chose to give. Open-ended questions can be used to probe subjects in depth and provide 'real' information rather than that which is

---

Box 9.2 Semantic scales

Semantic scales include:

- **Likert scales**, in which respondents state the extent to which they 'agree' or 'disagree' with a proposition. Typically they cover 'strongly disagree', 'disagree', 'neither agree nor disagree', 'agree' and 'strongly agree'. Such scales tend to be balanced in that they have a mid-point and an equal range on either side.
- **Semantic differential scales**, in which respondents record their opinions by marking a position on a scale defined by two extremes, such as 'large and small', 'honest and dishonest' or 'frequently and infrequently'.
- **Importance scales**, which measure customers' perceptions of the importance of a proposition by selecting from a scale which includes 'extremely important', 'very important', 'neither important or unimportant', 'not very important', 'not important at all'.

---

forced into a predetermined straightjacket. However, they also maximise the exposure to variations in interviewer interpretation of what respondents said, provide responses which vary from the monosyllabic to the verbose and can be extremely difficult to analyse if administered in large numbers.

Words

Whatever types of questions are used, the words which are used in questions are critical in determining whether the responses are accurate – and, more importantly, **consistent between respondents**. In ordinary speech the number of words can be increased in order to convey precisely the right message. In questionnaires, where space and time are limited, the correct meaning must be conveyed in a minimum number of words (Box 9.3). The need for complete unambiguity is heightened by the fact that questionnaires are normally applied by interviewers and not by the executive that has designed the questionnaire. It is unreasonable to rely on interviewer training and

---

Box 9.3 Words used on questionnaires

The main pitfalls in terms of the words used on questionnaires are:

- words which are **ambiguous**
- words which can **mean different things to different respondents**
- words which may be **offensive**
- words which **fail to capture the full range of options**
- **jargon and slang**
- wording which are **outside the normal experience** of the respondent

---

briefing to ensure that the responses are consistent, the first line of defence must be the questionnaire itself.

Ambiguous words are usually those which are vague or colloquial such as 'sort' instead of 'brand', 'like' instead of 'prefer', 'where' instead 'in which shop' or 'get' instead of 'purchase'. Examples of words which mean different things to different respondents include 'dinner', which could be either the midday or the evening meal depending on social group. Words which relate to race, sex, bodily functions, religion or even income may be unavoidable but have to be handled carefully to avoid giving offence. In some situations asking a respondent whether he or she is a 'Jew', as opposed to 'Jewish', would be taken as pejorative. A particular form of imprecision is the word which though accurate in itself fails to cover all of the possibilities. For example, if a product can be bought outright, leased or hired, asking respondents when they purchased may result in a negative response from those who leased or hired.

Jargon, technical language or slang is a major pitfall for questionnaire designers who have become so immersed in the subject-matter of the survey and the language used by suppliers that they fail to realise that they may be talking above the heads of the average respondents. This can be just as true in industrial surveys, where a higher level of technical knowledge could be expected, as in consumer surveys.

For researchers a particular problem arises when asking respondents to provide numerical responses. Because they are themselves numerate, words like percentage or proportion do not raise any problems, however, the average respondent who may have no particular difficulty in stating the number of purchases they made in a given period could be completely baffled by a request to state what proportions of their purchases were made in particular stores.

All wording needs to be matched to the experience level of the respondent. It may seem obvious that questionnaires designed for surveys of children need to use very simple words, but so may questionnaires designed for surveys of the elderly or low-income groups. In other situations simplicity could be taken as an insult to the respondent's intelligence. Although the problems with words can be considerable it is important to remember that they may be overcome by the context in which they are used and the introduction of supplementary explanations.

A survey carried out by the British Market Research Bureau[1] showed that one-quarter of the words used in a sample of questionnaires did not appear in Payne's list of 1000 most frequently used words. This suggests that designers of questionnaires tend to use words which are relatively unfamiliar to respondents. Generally unfamiliar words are acceptable if prior qualitative research indicates that they are understood by the particular audiences at which the questionnaire is aimed (e.g. computer terms in questionnaires designed for computer users), but if not they should be avoided.

Phrasing
In addition to using the correct words it is also necessary to ensure that the phrasing of questions is such that all respondents derive the same meaning from them. Any imprecision in the formation of questions can undermine the consistency of the results just as much as the use of imprecise words. Questions such as 'How many magazines have you purchased recently?' which permits respondents or interviewers to place different interpretations on what is meant by 'recent' will produce less accurate data than a question which asks 'How many magazines did you purchase in the last two weeks?'

Complex phrasing is a common problem and needs to be avoided, normally by breaking down the question into separate components. Questions such as 'Did you purchase product x from Sainsbury's during the last few weeks' might seem like a good way of getting to the point quickly but the accuracy of the results will be enhanced if the question is broken up into at least two separate questions, such as:

Did you purchase product x during the last four weeks?
From which of the following shops did you purchase it?

Similarly questions which require respondents to engage in mental arithmetic will produce responses of variable accuracy depending on their mental agility.

Bias
There are a wide range of terms which contain an in-built suggestion of virtue or opprobrium and are therefore likely to increase the levels of approval or disapproval thus biasing responses. 'Environmentally-friendly', 'green', 'home made', 'natural', or 'free range' all tend to be looked on favourably, whereas 'pollution', 'waste', 'pornography', 'disease' or 'poverty' would tend to induce feelings of hostility. Bias can also be induced by questions which permit respondents to anticipate the full question and 'jump the gun' when providing their answers. This can be avoided by ensuring that alternatives from which respondents have to choose are held back until a full explanation of the question has been given.

Leading questions
Leading questions are those in which the words or phrasing suggest an expected reply to the respondent. Often the element which leads the respondent is one of the words which bias respondents favourably or unfavourably as described above. Questions such as 'Are you in favour of restricting the amount of pornography on the internet?' will tend to produce positive responses even from those who avidly surf the net for erotic material. The problem can be enhanced in personal interviews because respondents are generally unwilling to expose their less acceptable predilections to a complete stranger. This fact has been used to explain a left-wing bias in opinion polls. Issues which are good for the community but

bad for some individuals, such as redistribution of income, receive excessively high approval ratings because of a widespread reluctance to admit to being a self-interested, right-wing bigot to the nice lady with the clipboard.

Order effects
Questions which rely on the presentation of alternatives to respondents need to take account of the fact that items presented first tend to receive a stronger reaction than those presented later. Questions which request a rating of the importance of a series of factors in determining their choice of product or supplier can result in higher scores for those listed first. This problem can be avoided by rotating the order in which items are listed.

Recall
The questionnaire must take into account the ability of respondents to recall what they did. Whereas respondents might be expected to recall the timing and circumstances of major purchases such as houses, cars or household appliances for some time, this would not be so for items which are purchased frequently such as food, personal hygiene and household items. For major purchases it could be reasonable to ask respondents to describe events over the previous 12 months; for frequently purchased items a week might be the maximum level of accurate recall that could be expected.

One method of overcoming the problem of recall is to ask respondents to consult their records of purchases. This is commonly used in industrial surveys where records are likely to be kept but is of value in consumer surveys only where individuals maintain records of their actions – such as banking, insurance, pensions or car maintenance. The need to consult records assumes that the interview is taking place where the records are kept but a more important problem is that respondents may regard a record search as too big an intrusion on their time or personal confidentially. Many who are prepared to respond in generalities will refuse to search for precise details.

Answerability
There are two issues relating to answerability. First will the respondent be **willing** answer; second will the respondent be **able** to answer? Willingness to respond can be effected by the sensitivity of the subject matter. The taboo areas (as with the wording problem described above) are commonly sex, income, personal hygiene, race and religion. Questions which are likely to arouse feelings of guilt may also encounter reluctance to respond. In contrast, subjects which are inherently interesting to respondents will be met with enthusiasm. Car clinics have little difficulty in gaining responses from car enthusiasts.

Ability to answer can be a function of whether the respondent has access to the facts (as in recall, above) or whether the expectations of the question are so complex that the respondent cannot comply. Perceived inability to answer can be as much of a problem as a genuine inability. Many respondents when asked to participate in a survey demonstrate a high level of uncertainty about their ability to do so, even on topics with which they are perfectly familiar. This sometimes stems from a fear that they will be made to look foolish or inadequate.

Questions which are almost certain to induce anxiety in a high proportion of respondents are those which include a requirement to make some form of calculations. Numeracy levels are such that there will inevitably be a significant proportion of respondents that will either make mistakes or will refuse to do the calculations, especially if they are required to do them in their heads and without the benefit of a calculator.[2]

Unwillingness to respond can be overcome by using good interviewers and by a survey introduction which emphasises that they are making a valuable contribution to a worthwhile enquiry. Genuine inability to respond needs to be highlighted in the initial screening questions and when encountered the respondents should be politely dropped. Perceived inability to respond requires assurances that all cooperation is worthwhile and that the experience will be painless or even enjoyable.

Assembling the questionnaire (Box 9.4)

Box 9.4 Key skills in assembling a questionnaire

The key skill in assembling the questions that are to asked into the full questionnaire are:

- **Question sequencing** – the first questions should be interesting and easy to answer. Respondents can be easily dissuaded from continuing if they feel that the exercise is a waste of time or that it will be too difficult. Difficult or highly personal questions should be positioned at the end of the questionnaire so that they arise when the respondent is confident and relaxed.
- **Logic** – the flow of questions should appear to be logical to the respondents. A sequence which switches irrationally from topic to topic will build up resentment among respondents.
- **Relevance** – the questions must be relevant to the respondents. Topics which appear to be unrelated to the objective of the interview will cause annoyance.
- **Refer-backs** – there is often a requirement to refer back to responses given in previous questions. These need to restricted to the minimum since they complicate the interview process and waste time. Respondents who are expected to wait whilst an interviewer works back through a questionnaire to find a previous answer can soon get bored and uncooperative.

- **Questionnaire length** – the length of the questionnaire will be driven by the number of topics to be covered, the research technique to be used and the relationship of the respondent to the research sponsor. Generally, short questionnaires achieve better response rates than long ones and are less likely to suffer from early termination. However, questionnaires that are to be applied by personal interview can normally be longer than those to be administered by telephone. The physical presence of the interviewer can normally stretch the attention span of the respondent. The shortest questionnaires are normally those which are self administered. Questionnaires which are applied to respondents that have an interest in the outcome of the survey or have a relationship with the survey sponsor that is likely to encourage them to respond (such as key account customers or employees) can afford to be longer than questionnaires that are to be applied to respondents that have minimal interest in the survey outcome or connection with the sponsor.
- **Format** – the physical presentation of the questionnaire must be conducive to easy administration and completion by the interviewers. Complex structures slow down the interview process. The format must have well defined grids on which to record answers, sufficient space for open-ended responses and clearly marked instructions, such as routeing to the next question to be asked if the printed sequence needs to be altered.
- **Insertion of correct routeing instructions** – questionnaire often include questions which do not apply to all respondents and need to be omitted depending on the responses given to previous questions. A questionnaire which commences with 'Do you own an automobile?' may have two separate sets of questions depending on whether the response is 'yes' or 'no'. There may then be separate sets of questions for owners of each make of car or for the years in which the cars were purchased. The routeing instructions ensure that respondents are channelled to the questions which are relevant to them.
- **Other interviewer instructions** – the interview process frequently requires the interviewer to take specific actions such as show display materials, probe on specific topics or communicate additional information. These need to be added to the questionnaire at the appropriate point as a reminder to the interviewers. Instructions may also be required to ensure that interviewers record the responses in a manner which is clear and consistent.

Piloting the questionnaires

Once designed, it is advisable to test a questionnaire by carrying out a series of pilot interviews with a small sample of respondents. Pilot interviews are carried out to test:

- whether all questions can be answered and that respondents are likely to be willing to answer them

- that all questions can be answered by a single respondent
- that the questionnaire flows logically and is ordered in a way which respondents find easy to follow
- that precoded questions include all major options
- that the questionnaire is not too long.

Approving the questionnaire

The critical importance of the questionnaire in the research process means that it is essential to agree its content with the management that is expecting to make use of the survey results prior to the full-scale launch of the survey. Management will not be expert in questionnaire design but they will be able to comment on content (missing or superfluous questions) and terminology. They may also be in a position to comment on whether respondents will be in a position to provide answers to questions and whether the wording is likely to be ambiguous.

9.2 Self-completion questionnaires

Not all questionnaires are applied by interviewers. Some are sent by mail or fax or are placed on the internet for completion by respondents themselves. In these situations the need for clarity, unambiguity and simplicity are enhanced since there is nobody available to explain points which are unclear. There is an argument in favour of the removal of the interviewer on the grounds that it can eliminate interviewer-induced bias, but this is offset by the importance of the interviewer in encouraging response. At a more technical level, self-completion provide respondents with the opportunity to take more time to consider their responses. They can also read through the entire questionnaire before answering. Although more time for consideration and a thorough reading of the questionnaire could be regarded as a plus point it could also bias the responses because the respondent has time to work out the objectives of the survey.

Where self-completion questionnaires are used, design can have a major influence on the willingness of respondents to participate in the survey. The main disincentives to participation are:

- questionnaires which are too long
- questionnaires which are too complex
- questions which are obviously ambiguous
- too many questions which respondents are unable or unwilling to answer
- questions which are perceived as boring
- surveys which are perceived as futile or wasteful of respondents' time.

9.3 **Questionnaire layout**

Questionnaires do not necessarily need to have a high-quality appearance – unless they are self-completed, in which case high-quality appearance may encourage response – but they must be set out so that they are **efficient and effective tools for data capture**. Hard-copy questionnaires are not only the means of asking questions but also the vehicle for recording responses. In addition to a clean easy-to-read format they also need to have:

- enough space for recording responses to open-ended questions
- shading, boxes and grid patterns to ensure that responses are aligned with the questions to which they refer
- prompts and probes printed in bold so they catch in the eye of the interviewer
- single-side printing so that questionnaires do not have to be turned over.

In addition there are a wide range of options to increase interview quality and facilitate analysis. These include the use of colour pages to denote different types of respondents, and the use of colour or shading in the questionnaire to denote questions that are of particular importance.

9.4 **Computer-Aided Interviews**

Computer-aided interviews[3] solve many of the mechanical problems outlined above. Questionnaire routeing, refer-backs, verification of responses and questionnaire completion are all facilitated to a considerable extent by computerisation. The physical task of questionnaire creation is more complex, since it is required to cope with data entry as well as the questioning itself, but the basic skills in question design are identical to those outlined above. However, it is important to remember that no amount of computer technology will convert a bad question into a good question.

9.5 **Interest and Relevance**

'Research fatigue' is a growing problem amongst certain respondent groups that tend to be over-researched. It is most evident in industry where some segments, such as users of information technology (IT) and communications equipment, have been subjected to a large number of surveys.

Respondents' willingness to cooperate in surveys is partly a function of the level of enthusiasm and interest that can be raised in advance of and during the interview process. Whilst this is heavily influenced by the subject-matter of the survey, the questionnaire can also make an important contribution, particularly in stopping respondents from cutting short their participation before the questionnaire is completed. The two major concerns of respondents when approached to participate in surveys are:

- Do I really want to be bothered?
- Am I the right person to ask?

The introductory statements on the questionnaire need to anticipate both of these problems by setting out the reasons for the survey, the types of respondents that are eligible to respond and the fact that each respondent's contribution will provide a valuable input to the client's marketing programme and will ultimately bring some benefits to consumers. From then on it is down to the questionnaire to make the interview process as quick, unobtrusive and interesting as possible. Although it is difficult to make an inherently boring subject interesting, time must be spent on ensuring that the pitfalls which antagonise respondents are avoided. Length, flow, repetition, irrelevance and confusion can all make interviews tedious and will build resistance to cooperation. Computer-based questionnaires (other than those applied by telephone) have the in-built advantage of being able to add graphics and sound which can be used creatively to hold respondents' attention.

Notes

1   John O'Brien, 'How do Market Researchers Ask Questions?', *Journal of the Market Research Society*, 26(2) (1984).
2   See Norman Webb, 'Levels of Adult Numeracy', *Journal of the Market Research Society*, 26(2) (1984).
3   Described in detail in Chapter 11.

10 Conventional Primary Research Techniques

Although it can be a prolific source of data, secondary research is rarely enough for marketing problem solving. This means that most projects make use of primary research techniques to collect original data from participants in markets. The main advantage of primary research is that it can be directed at all types of respondents that possess information and can ask questions which are directly relevant to the problem in hand. The main disadvantage is that primary research is inevitably expensive. It therefore needs to be planned carefully, particularly with respect to the techniques that are used, in order to ensure that data is collected cost effectively (Box 10.1).

All primary research involves direct contact with respondents using a questionnaire or an interview guide and sometimes requiring display material or samples of the product being researched.

Box 10.1 Primary research techniques

The major primary research techniques currently in use for marketing research are:

- Personal (face-to-face) interviews
- Telephone interviews
- Group discussions (focus groups)
- Self-completion questionnaires
- Diaries
- Product tests
- Observation techniques
- Projective techniques
- Mystery shopping.

10.1 The Interview

Whether carried out face-to-face or by telephone, the interview is the most common data collection technique used in market research. It seeks

---

Box 10.2 Personal interviews

- **Advantages:**
  - Depth coverage of subjects
  - Ability to show and handle materials
  - Facts can be verified by reference to sources
  - Visual verification of respondent characteristics
  - Observations of respondent reactions.

- **Disadvantages:**
  - Relatively high cost
  - Difficult/costly to reach random samples
  - Requirement to book appointments (sometimes)
  - Higher intrusion on respondent time reduces willingness to respond

---

information on respondents' actions, reactions, preferences, perceptions or requirements. It can be carried out in a variety of locations of which the most common are the street, the home, the place of work or a specific venue associated with the research topic, such as a shop, in an airport or on a train. The live contact between the interviewer and the respondent permits not only data collection but also the verification of responses and the introduction of supplementary questions to probe the unusual or unexpected. An advantage of face-to-face interviews is that they can be set up to permit subjects to be explored in depth – in which case they are called 'depth personal interviews' (Box 10.2).

Personal interviewing can be:

- one-on-one
- paired
- family interviews
- triangular.

Most commonly personal interviews are with one person at a time. For more depth analysis, however, it is possible to interview couples – normally a husband and wife, an entire family unit or three people who represent opposing points of view. Couple and family interviews permit the exploration of **shared decisions**, such as purchases of household durables or cars. Triangular interviews represent mini-group discussions and provide some of the advantages described below for that technique, but at significantly lower cost.

As telephone ownership has become universal, telephone research has tended to displace personal interviewing, largely because it is quicker, can be controlled better and is less expensive. The telephone is ideally suited to the collection of small amounts of highly structured information from samples that are scattered over a wide geographical area. It is unsuitable for individuals who are unlikely to respond well on the telephone, such as

---

Box 10.3 Telephone interviewing

- **Advantages:**
  - Relatively low cost
  - Easy to reach random samples
  - Less time commitment required from respondents
  - Can be applied internationally from central interview base.

- **Disadvantages:**
  - No ability to observe respondents
  - Difficult to show materials during the interview
  - Limited interview time (30 minutes max.)
  - Easier for respondents to refuse interviews.

---

children, or those that are difficult to reach by telephone, such as residents in old people's homes or farmers; nor can it be used when material needs to be displayed to the respondents. The telephone can be less intrusive than personal interviews but can also be unwelcome during the evenings, the time when respondents are most likely to be at home.

For business research the telephone can be the most acceptable method of data collection because it requires the least time commitment by respondents.

The main disadvantages of telephone research are the lack of visual contact, which means that respondents' reactions cannot be observed, and the relative ease with which respondents can refuse to cooperate (Box 10.3).

The data collected by personal and telephone interviews is exposed to a risk of bias introduced by the interviewers. Bias potentially arises from:

- interviewers inadvertently leading respondents to a **preferred response** by the way in which questions are asked, tone of voice or facial expression; there are a number of ways in which an interviewer can suggest approval for a particular reply
- interviewers hearing what they **expect** rather than what the respondents actually say; a common problem when interviewers carry out a large number of interviews on a single project
- respondents adjusting their replies to conform with what they feel the interviewer **expects to hear**; this can happen either because of a social incompatibility between the interviewer and the respondent, the nature of the questioning or a desire to avoid further questioning.

10.2 Group discussions (Focus Groups)

Group discussions are face-to-face interviews carried out with a collected group of respondents. Though difficult and expensive to organise, they yield

---

Box 10.4 Group discussions

- **Advantages:**
  - In-depth probing of topics
  - Interaction between participants
  - Ability to show products and visual aids
  - User of the research can view the process.

- **Disadvantages:**
  - High cost
  - Difficult to organise
  - Time-consuming to organise
  - High risk that respondents will not attend
  - Requires above-average interviewing (moderation) skills.

---

massive amounts of qualitative information, enhanced by the fact that participants can argue and debate between themselves. The moderation of such events is a skilled process but, done well, a few groups of six–eight participants can reveal far more about customers' requirements or attitudes than the equivalent 12–16 interviews. Groups can be used only with respondents that can be brought together physically, commonly in specialy designed rooms with video, sound recording and viewing facilities. This is rarely a problem with consumer groups where there are usually enough qualifying respondents living in the catchment area of the facility, but it can become more problematical for more widely dispersed respondents such as purchasing officers or surgeons. Part of the added cost of group discussion research arises from the fact that participants are commonly remunerated for the time they have devoted to take part in the group (Box 10.4).

The recruitment of groups is a skilled and demanding process. Getting a single respondent to cooperate at a convenient time can be difficult enough but getting up to eight respondents who all fulfil the selection criteria together in the same place at the same time can sometimes seem impossible. The process is commonly undertaken by freelance researchers who specialise in the recruitment of groups in their region.

10.3 The Self-completion Questionnaire

Self-completion questionnaires are either:

- mailed
- faxed
- handed out to respondents
- collected by respondents for self-completion and return to the researcher.

This is a low-cost research technique still used in social research but of declining importance in commercial market research. Self-completion questionnaires have a value in extracting information from respondents that are difficult to contact by other methods, such as executives constantly on the move, or in situations where respondents can be identified but it is not feasible to carry out an interview on the spot – as in traffic surveys, for example.

The main problem with self-completion questionnaires is the lack of control over the response. Response rates tend to be low and it is difficult if not impossible to demonstrate that those who choose to reply are typical of the universe as a whole. The most extreme example is the guest questionnaire placed in hotel bedrooms which are invariably completed only if the guest wishes to register a complaint.

In business research, faxing questionnaires injects an element of urgency which can be missing in postal surveys. Faxed questionnaires can also be as effective as the telephone in their ability to reach the targeted respondent (a major weakness in mail surveys which too often end in the postroom waste bin along with 'junk mail'). Unfortunately, domestic fax ownership is too low for this technique to be useful for consumer surveys (Box 10.5).

Box 10.5 Mail/fax questionnaires

- **Advantages:**
  - Low cost
  - Respondent can complete in his/her own time
  - Display material can be included (mail).

- **Disadvantages:**
  - Lack of control over response
  - Commonly low response rates
  - High risk of bias
  - Limited ability to follow up on statements
  - Short questionnaire.

The advantages of faxed questionnaires are that they replace printing and postage costs with (lower) line charges. They also avoid the complex and time-consuming process of collating and folding questionnaires and stuffing them into envelopes. Finally, they reach the respondents quickly and can be returned quickly. The disadvantages are that they look less attractive than printed questionnaires, they cannot enclose an incentive, they can be subject to transmission errors and – by imposing a charge on the recipient for the paper (however trivial that may seem) and the return costs, they can cause some antagonism and reluctance to respond. Dickson and Maclachlan[1] suggest eight situations in which fax surveys are more appropriate than mail surveys:

- the population to be surveyed has near universal fax ownership
- the questionnaires do not require high-quality images
- respondents can give the return fax to an assistant to return, thus avoiding time spent at the fax machine
- the study does not benefit greatly from enclosing incentives
- faxed returns do not go to a line which is too busy
- respondents are not concerned about junk faxes
- the return costs do not matter to the respondents
- the survey does not contain sensitive questions.

In a test of fax and mailed questionnaires to comparable respondents it has been shown[2] that fax surveys do in fact obtain higher and faster response rates than mailed questionnaires.

10.4 Diaries

Diaries are used in surveys which seek to track respondents' actions over a period of time. The diary is, in effect, a questionnaire on which the respondent records his or her purchases daily, weekly or monthly, depending on the nature of the survey. Diaries are placed with respondents at the commencement of the survey and collected once the diary period is completed. Diaries can run for a fixed calender period or can be completed once a target number of transactions or events are recorded.

Diaries demand a high degree of commitment from respondents to ensure that the data is regularly, comprehensively and accurately entered. Commitment can be gained by some form of compensation (cash or prizes in a competition) and by engaging the respondents more deeply in the objectives and outcome of the survey. Diaries are most commonly, though not exclusively, used on panel surveys for which panel members agree to submit data for relatively long periods of time (six months or a year). In these situations panel members join a 'club' which distributes newsletters and offers regular incentives in order to ensure continuous cooperation.

Diaries require above-average skills in drafting in order to ensure that they capture the data required accurately and can be completed easily by respondents. In some cases the diaries can provide a direct benefit to respondents by helping them to keep track of their transactions. In research terms this also gives rise to a problem since the observation of such information may begin to bias respondents purchasing habits and make them **untypical of the market as a whole**. For this reason, the diary method can be used for only limited periods of time.

10.5 **Product Tests**

Product tests (sometimes referred to as hall tests) are an experimental technique used in new product development programmes when samples of the products need to be shown to or tested on samples of potential buyers. They comprise a physical set-up in a facility or hall, commonly located in or near a shopping precinct. Respondents are recruited to visit the facility, test the product and record their reactions.

10.6 **Observation Techniques**

Observation encompasses a wide range of research techniques ranging from measured reactions to products or advertising material to recording the ways in which customers shop, handle products or behave and to the physical exmination of competitors' products. In customer research observation is a **physical**, as opposed to a reported, record of customer actions and can therefore be more accurate. It can also provide data which no amount of customer research can provide. Suppliers regularly engage in 'reverse engineering' in order to determine how competitors are formulating or designing their products. This involves obtaining an example of the product and dismantling it or subjecting it to chemical analysis.

Specialist observation techniques are used in experimental research but most observation research involves simple records of what is seen going on in a market.

Laboratory research

As its name implies, laboratory research involves observing customers in a laboratory or controlled environment in which **external influences are eliminated**. This permits precise measurement of the effects of the research objects on samples of customers. Different stimuli can be used with different matched samples so that the effect of the changes can be measured. Unfortunately the situations in which customers are observed are often artificial and their reactions may differ from those in real life. Nevertheless the techniques permit the collection of data which would be difficult, if not impossible to acquire by any other research approaches.

In the most common laboratory exercises, images of products, packaging, advertisements and other marketing materials are displayed to samples of customers whose reactions are measured physically (Box 10.6).

Marketplace observations

Less complex observation techniques involve the collection of data by watching and recording the actions of shoppers, distributors or suppliers as

---

Box 10.6 Experimental exercises

Such experiments include the use of:

- **Tachistoscope (T-Scope)**, a slide projector with a facility to project images for precise periods of time (normally fractions of a second) and with the capability of doing so at varied levels of light; tachistoscope tests are used primarily to test the visual impact of advertisements (by showing the levels of exposure at which headlines and key words are recognised) and the effectiveness with which advertisements communicate information (by determining the amount of the message which audiences can recall after defined lengths of display).
- **Brain wave analysis**, in which the interest generated by marketing materials is measured via the brain wave patterns they create.
- **Eye tracking**, which uses a device to track and measure the amount of time respondents spend on each part of an advertisement or package and to show the sequence with which parts are examined.
- **Psychogalvanometers**, which measure emotional reactions to images or messages by measuring changes in the rate of perspiration.
- **Voice pitch analysis**, which tests response by measuring changes in the pitch of respondents voices.

---

they go about their normal business. It is possible to record a wide range of useful information including the actions of shoppers as they pass through retail outlets, the production resources used by manufacturers, distribution practices of suppliers, the amount of shelf space allocated to projects and brands in shops and the types of staff used to provide customer service. This type of observation needs to be covert but has the advantage of recording **real situations** rather than the artificial ones that are created in laboratory experiments.

10.7 **Projective techniques**

Qualitative research makes use of a number of projective techniques which have been borrowed from clinical psychology (Box 10.7). Many regard them as being of limited usefulness but there are situations in which they can elicit descriptions of concepts which would not be achievable by other means. They may also be great fun to apply!

Projective techniques require highly skilled interviewers and are therefore expensive to complete. The findings therefore tend to be based on small samples which are subject to high margins of error. Respondents may also have difficulty in playing the game, particularly if they are attempted in professional and industrial buying situations.

Box 10.7 Key projective techniques

The key projective techniques that are available are:

- **Word association tests** – in which the repondent is asked to state the words which come to mind when a single word is mentioned; can be of some value in advertising research.
- **Sentence completion** – in which respondents are asked to complete a sentence such as 'Flying XYZ airline is . . .'; can reveal attitudes towards companies, products and brands.
- **TAT (Thematic Apperception Tests)** – in which respondents are asked to describe the characteristics of a person featured in a cartoon drawing of a market situation.
- **Cartoons** – respondents are presented with cartoon characters one of which is making a statement in a balloon and the other has a blank balloon; the respondent is required to fill in what they feel is an appropriate response in the empty balloon.

10.8 Mystery Shopping

In mystery shopping exercises (or Mystery Customers' Research, MCR) interviewers **pose as customers** in order to monitor staff performance and test the practice and effectiveness of service provision. The technique is widely used by retailers, banks, operators of public houses and restaurants and suppliers of services, such as public transport and financial advice, to determine whether company and sales procedures are being followed. It is also used as a source of competitive intelligence by shopping for rival services. The ethics of the technique have been challenged on the grounds that it involves deception, commonly uses secret taping of respondents and the fact that the respondents, whose time is unwittingly taken up, may lose revenue as a result of their participation in the exercise. These objections can be overcome, at least in part, by advising staff members that a mystery shopping exercise is in progress, by arranging some form of compensation for lost income or, where practical, by asking the mystery shopper to make a purchase. Despite the ethical objections, mystery shopping is one of the most rapidly growing research activities, illustrating that what research users find most useful does not always equate with that which the research business is comfortable providing.

10.9 Response and Refusal Rates

Response and refusal rates are a growing problem with all forms of primary research. This is not only because it may make the research more expensive but also because it can compromise the accuracy of the sample. In some cases, resistance to cooperation is due to 'respondent fatigue', as in the industry sectors such as telecommunications and information technology which have been over-researched in recent years. It can also be due to growing cynicism amongst respondents following some high-profile research exposure, such as the opinion polls and reports of focus groups being used to define political policies. It is also caused by increasing publicity being given to data protection legislation.

In industrial research refusal rates are increasing as it becomes more difficult to reach respondents by telephone. The use of voicemail to filter calls also makes it considerably easier for respondents to refuse to accept calls from market researchers.

Notes

1   John Dickson and Douglas Maclachlan, 'Fax Surveys: Return Patterns and Comparison with Mail Surveys', *Journal of Marketing Research*, 33(2) (1996).
2   Ibid.

11 Electronic Data Collection

Electronic data collection techniques have spread their influence throughout research and have come into their own as hardware costs have reduced significantly, computer ownership proliferated, low-cost, high-powered laptop computers have become available and software has become increasingly user-friendly. The range of devices and systems in current use includes:

- Computer-aided telephone interviewing systems (CATI)
- Computer-aided personal interviewing systems (CAPI)
- Computer-aided self-administered interviewing systems (CASI)
- Disk-based questionnaires
- Optically read questionnaires
- Automated voice questionnaires
- EPOS systems
- Electronic meters
- 'Smart' credit and bank cards
- Voting systems
- Video conference focus groups
- High-tech observation techniques

There is in addition the major research potential offered by the internet which is covered separately in Chapter 12.

Electronics have been used in research virtually since they first became available. The need to process large volumes of data meant that survey research was an early user of computers and since then researchers have been particularly inventive in adapting a variety of electronic products and processes to their requirements. However, the development of electronic data capture techniques provided the greatest spur to the use of electronics in research. The advantages they offer in terms of high levels of reliability and reduced cost coupled with the fact that they can in some situations replace interviewers – always regarded as the weakest link in the research process – has led to a rapid increase in their use.

Despite the advantages, electronic data capture techniques are highly unlikely to replace interviewers completely. They require a high level of prior structuring and are therefore generally unacceptable for qualitative research where the interaction between moderators (or depth interviewers) and respondents is too deep and detailed to permit any form of anticipation of what is likely to occur. Indeed, the entire point of qualitative research is to probe the unknown and if enough was known to set up the questionnaire the research would be unnecessary. Even for quantitative research electronic techniques require considerable time, and therefore cost, to set up. Although set-up costs are reducing, electronic techniques are viable only when the savings per interview are sufficiently high to cover the set-up costs.

11.1 CATI, CAPI and CASI Systems

The most widespread form of automation in research are the CATI, CAPI and CASI systems which computerise the collection of information in the form of screen-based questionnaires (Box 11.1).

The management system associated with CATI interviews holds a file of potential respondents and ensures that the quotas of different respondent types are maintained.

CATI systems (Box 11.2) were the first computer-aided interviews to be introduced. The software and computer power required to run them became available on mainframe systems in the 1980s and proved their worth in large sample surveys of consumers. Over time they migrated to desk-top PCs and falling costs have made them accessible to all research organisations. Increased simplicity of the software has also meant that whereas previously

---

Box 11.1 Computer-aided interviews

These sophisticated programmes:

- Display the questionnaire on a screen
- Display sound, pictures and video to which a reaction is required (as in advertisement testing) or simply to improve interest levels
- Capture the responses via the keyboard
- Verify each response (to ensure that it is compatible with other responses given)
- Ensure that all questions are completed
- Insert the correct 'skip' patterns (i.e. eliminate questions which respondents are not required to answer)
- Randomise lists of products or attributes so that order effects are eliminated
- Relate questions in later parts of the questionnaire to responses given earlier on (e.g. 'You stated that you purchased a product manufactured by X, can you tell me which of the following models you bought?)
- Filter out particular responses which need to be subject to open-ended probing (e.g. 'You rated product X higher than the others on its design, can you please tell me what it is about the design that you particularly like?)
- Prepare the data for instant analysis.

Box 11.2 CATI systems

CATI systems simplify the research process by:

- distributing respondent names and telephone numbers automatically to the next available interviewer in the telephone interview centre
- re-presenting partially completed interviews which have been interrupted for some reason, to an interviewer for completion at a time nominated by the respondent
- closing down categories of respondents once the quotas have been filled.

---

the set-up time, and therefore costs, were so high that they were viable only in large-scale surveys, they can now be used even when the interview numbers are low.

For widespread application, CAPI and CASI interviews have had to await the availability of low-cost, low-weight, high-speed, keyboard or pen-based laptops, palmtops and touch screen computers. They are in effect an electronic version of the paper questionnaire but they share the data entry, verification and analysis advantages of CATI systems. CAPI systems are questionnaires loaded on laptop or notepad computers which are carried by interviewers instead of the traditional paper questionnaires. Whilst they are not suitable for all interview locations, particularly wet and windy street corners, when they can be used they facilitate the interviewers' task just as effectively as the in-house CATI systems.

CASI systems extend the benefits of electronic systems to self-completion interviews (Box 11.3).[1] For obvious reasons, the use of the laptop or touch screen computer has to be supervised and CASI systems are not an alternative to mailed questionnaires. CASI systems not only improve the quality of the responses but also make self-completion a more interesting, and therefore more acceptable process for respondents, compared with paper and pencil questionnaires. They can be set up at locations to which the target respondents are invited or at which they are likely to congregate – such as waiting rooms in hospitals. A major application is in hall tests or clinics, such as those used to test consumer reaction to new car designs.

11.2 Disk-based Questionnaires

Wider ownership of PCs, particularly in offices, has given birth to disk-based questionnaires. In this approach, questionnaires, together with graphics and screen presentations, are loaded on floppy disk and mailed or distributed to respondents for self-completion. They offer many of the advantages of CAPI and CATI systems and eliminate the cost of an interviewer. The novel approach also increases the likelihood that they will

---

Box 11.3 CASI systems

The users of CASI systems must take account of some additional factors not relevant to CATI and CAPI systems which are administered by professional interviewers:

- The study organiser must ensure that the respondents either have sufficient keyboard skills to enter the responses or be sufficiently comfortable with computers to use light pens or touch-screens. This may be more of a problem with certain respondent groups than others.
- As with all self-completion questionnaires, particular attention must be paid to questionnaire design to ensure that it is not confusing. The key word is 'consistency' – scales should all run the same way and instructions should be in the same type face and colour.
- The fonts used must be large enough to be read easily on a small screen, since space is not a limitation this should not pose any problem.
- The number of keyboard actions required by the respondent should be minimised; completed responses should automatically bring up the next question
- The progress to a new question must be obvious; respondents can be easily confused by questionnaires which contain a number of similar questions and repeat their responses thinking that the question has not changed
- The correction of responses later felt to be inaccurate or those where an incorrect response is given inadvertently, must be easy
- The number of remaining questions should be made evident to the respondents; this can be judged easily on paper questionnaires but not on a computer system
- Responses should be saved frequently.

---

be completed and returned. The main disadvantage is that their use is limited to situations where a high proportion of the universe to be researched has access to a PC and is 'computer literate'. At present this tends to restrict them to business research where they have been used for surveys on information technology.

11.3 Optically Read Questionnaires

Fully structured questionnaires on which responses can be indicated by ticks or marks lend themselves to analysis by optical mark readers and have gained some use in the research industry. Their main advantages are their ease of application and the simplicity and speed with which they can be scanned and analysed. The cost of setting up the questionnaires and the analysis means that sample sizes need to be substantial in order to justify the use of this technique.

11.4 **Automated Voice Questionnaires**

Automated voice questionnaires, or Interactive Voice Responses (IVR), require respondents to call a computer centre and be led through a completely automated interview. Respondents hear a recorded set of questions and signify their responses by pressing keys on their telephone. The software permits routeing of questions depending on answers given and the entry of spoken comments which are recorded for later transcription. The technique has all the charisma and warmth of a 'speak your weight' machine, but it eliminates the requirement for interviewers and permits respondents to enter their responses at a time to suit themselves. However, like all self-administered techniques it reduces the amount of control that the research staff have over the sample and the individual respondents and thereby suffers from some of the disadvantages of self-completion questionnaires which are completed manually.

The future development of IVR is likely to be through speech recognition systems which can capture and analyse spoken responses to all questions.

11.5 **EPOS Systems**

Scanners and stock control systems which collect point of sale and stock information have proved to be of considerable value in tracking the flow of products through distributors. The analysis of tapes obtained from retailers and wholesalers has replaced physical store checks for many product groups. This approach is far from inexpensive, since retailers have discovered the value of the data they collect and therefore charge for it, but it does offer the possibility of tracking a high proportion of the products which are sold by various categories of retailer, thus minimising the exposure to sampling error.

Scanners in stores provide the opportunity to link store throughput with the **demographics of the consumers making the purchases** – a traditional weakness of retail audits. This complex approach requires the recruitment of a panel of stores, which are equipped with modified scanners, *and* a panel of households from whom demographic details are collected. The household panel members have identification numbers which are recorded at the checkout to link their purchases with their demographic characteristics. The analysis of this data provides information which is comparable to that obtained from consumer panels.

A major problem with the scanner technique is convincing retailers to permit the use of their own tapes for research purposes or to participate in panel surveys. Even when the windfall financial gain is high, some retailers refuse to cooperate and, if their share of market is significant, the findings require substantial adjustment in order to make them representative of the market as a whole.

Scanners are also used in consumer panel surveys as a partial replacement for manually recorded diary data. Hand-held scanners are used to record the bar codes on packages purchased.

11.6 Electronic Meters

Electronic meters are widely used in television audience research to collect viewing statistics. Current versions record the times a representative sample of television sets are switched on and off, the channels tuned and, via a sensor system, the number of individuals watching the set. This data is collected automatically through a telephone link to a central computer for overnight analysis. The cost of the meters and the associated communications systems and software which permit the data they collect to be downloaded to a central computer overnight for analysis the following day represent a highly capital-intensive research system which can be employed only where there is substantial demand for the data and a high value attachment to the findings.

The use of meters for other research measurements which lend themselves to mechanical analysis, such as the running times, speeds, gear changes and the number of starts and stops of vehicles, have been explored but not, as yet, implemented on any significant scale. However, the use of intelligent metering for billing purposes such as in electricity, gas and water provides a mechanism for data collection as a by-product and will be used increasingly as a research resource by suppliers of products which are sold on a metered basis.

11.7 'Smart' Credit and Bank Cards

The introduction of 'smart' credit and bank cards which can relate product or service purchases with the source of purchase, the price paid and the demographics of the purchaser will provide a complementary data collection resource to EPOS systems in the near future.

11.8 Voting Systems

Voting systems, provide members of an audience or a group discussion with a push-button device on which they can record their selection ('yes', 'no' or one a series of numbered options). They are used to provide instant reactions to propositions. The software provides a read-out of the proportions of the audience or group members voting for each option and the systems are of greatest value when there is a requirement for continuous, anonymous measurement of changes in attitude as sessions progress.

11.9 Video Conference Focus Groups

A major disadvantage of focus groups is that it is difficult, or expensive, to bring together respondents that live or work long distances from each other. This may mean that the quality of the group is compromised by the fact that participation is limited to respondents in a small geographical region. Whilst this is unlikely to be a severe problem with consumer groups, it can prove a significant disadvantage in the case of industrial or professional groups where the number of suitable respondents is limited and they may not work in close proximity to each other. Telephone conferencing has provided a partial solution to this problem but is not ideal because a substantial part of the benefit of observing a group is derived from seeing the expressions and body language of the participants. Video conferencing is a much better method of increasing the geographical coverage of a single group. Its application has been limited by high cost and the poor quality of the video conference signals. The introduction of ISDN lines, which speed up data transmission sufficiently to overcome signal problems, makes video conference focus groups a more practical proposition from a technical standpoint whilst the rapid reduction in telecommunications costs are helping to make them a feasible proposition from a financial point of view.

11.10 High-tech Observation Techniques

The latest addition to observation techniques is the commercial satellite image.[2] Of greatest value in competitive intelligence, high-resolution digital satellite images can show:

- plant layout
- external processes
- transport facilities
- external stocks
- new plant construction

Images can also be used to track changes month by month or year by year. Current satellite technology can show objects down to the size of a large lawnmower. Satellite images were developed for military applications but are soon to be made available commercially by a number of vendors.

Notes

1   See Mike Curtis, 'Putting Handheld CASI to the Test in an Automotive Consumer Clinic', paper presented at InterCASIC '96, The International Conference on Computer-Assisted Survey Information Collection (San Antonio Texas, December 1996).
2   See Fred Wergeles, 'Commercial Satellite Imagery – New Opportunities for Competitive Intelligence', *Competitive Intelligence Magazine*, 1(1) (1998).

12 Market Research on the Internet

The internet is, in principle, the answer to a market analyst's prayer. Many of the tasks that can be carried out on the internet could almost have been designed with market research in mind. As a massive showcase of data and as an effective and low-cost mechanism for collecting information on any topic and from any point of the globe, the internet represents a resource with which no traditional library can conceivably compete. As a method of sending and receiving text, images and voice messages to and from any individual, commercial organisation, government body or institution that is connected, the internet has the potential to displace many of the traditional primary data collection techniques. The process has already begun but the internet still suffers from serious flaws which limit its applications in market research. These will be solved over time and the research industry will certainly adopt the internet as an important tool in its armoury of research techniques. One of the biggest spurs is solving the problems will be the need for truly global research techniques to meet the requirements of global marketing. The internet, like the telephone, has the facility to globalise data collection.

12.1 What is the Internet?

The internet was born in the 1960s as a means of linking various defence-related scientific projects being carried out in universities in the USA. The Advanced Research Projects Agency established ARPAnet as a national network of computers which would permit rapid communication and data transfer between the scientific researchers and academics working on its projects. It continued as a US government project linking a limited number of computers until the 1980s. In 1982 a new network addressing system, which permitted the link-up of thousands of computers, was introduced and the internet as we know it came into being. From this point on the internet developed rapidly outside government and academic sectors. Corporate users were among the first to appreciate its potential but the real explosion began when internet access providers made available the mechanisms for low-cost local connections by private individuals world-wide.

12.2 **The Internet as a Research Tool**

The internet features which are of most value to market researchers are:

- e-mail
- discussion forums
- file transfer protocol (FTP)
- newsgroups
- online service providers
- the World Wide Web.

The first five of these are offered by the organisations providing internet access, using the internet itself as a means of communication. The last is the vast and ever-expanding network of web sites that can be accessed from the internet.

E-mail

Electronic mail is a system for transferring messages and files from computer to computer regardless of where they are in the world. E-mail is gradually replacing the fax as the favoured electronic communication method, just as the fax, in its day, replaced the telex. The major advantage of e-mail is that text and images sent can be downloaded into the recipient's software, worked on at a time convenient to the respondent, returned and analysed. The advantages for survey research are obvious and there is the added bonus that an e-mail questionnaire can include colour images of products or advertisements for respondents to comment on – though, at present, these are unlikely to be regarded by advertisers as being of sufficient quality for a reliable advertisement test. The use of e-mail as a data collection technique is also relatively fresh and likely to produce a more positive reaction than telephone, postal or faxed questionnaires. Doubtless this advantage will come to an end as 'junk e-mail' increases the level of resistance to unsolicited and unwelcome messages.

Discussion forums

Discussion forums are computerised meeting places in which those interested in the topic covered by the forum can exchange messages and information and gain access to files. Each forum tends to cover a single topic and can include a message section, file libraries and a conference room. Joining a forum provides you with the facility to observe what is going on within it, obtain information and ask questions.

Message sections
Message sections can be used for obtaining answers to questions on any topic from others entering the forum. Since these are likely to be individuals

with an interest in the topic, the chances of obtaining an informed response are high.

File libraries
File libraries are offered by a wide range of organisations – most notably, but far from exclusively, the manufacturers of computer equipment and software who use them to provide support for their products. A search through the forums will identify what is available and a full list of the files that can be downloaded (using FTP, see below) plus a description of what they contain.

Conference rooms
As the name suggests, conference rooms provide a facility for online conversations with others in the forum. They provide a similar service to the message section but without the wait.

The usefulness of discussion forums varies depending on whether one exists for the topic of interest, who can be accessed and their level of knowledge. However, as the number of internet connections expands, forums provide an interesting alternative to a telephone search for expertise and are likely to become an important resource for business intelligence.

FTP

FTP provides the facility to transfer files from one part of the internet to another, enabling users to collect files from organisations that have agreed to make them available. FTP represents an alternative to the file libraries within the forums described above, though relatively few are of direct relevance to researchers. Furthermore, the process can be slow and a certain amount of expertise and imagination is required to determine where files are and which files are likely to provide the information that is required.

Newsgroups (or bulletin boards)

Newsgroups provide another method of communicating with special interest groups, of which there are hundreds of thousands already on the net and new ones being added by the minute. Relevant newsgroups can be identified by using a **keyword search** in the newsreader programme offered by the internet service provider. Messages or questions can be posted into a relevant newsgroup in the expectation that they will be read by thousands of people world-wide and that valuable responses will be obtained. The responses are 'threaded' in that they contain the original question plus all the responses and comments that have been made together with the signatures of each person providing a contribution. This tends to make the files extremely large but enables the reader to follow the various threads of the discussion that has taken place. Some groups are edited by an individual who chooses to receive all the responses and decide what is added to the file.

As with forums, the usefulness of a newsgroup depends on the calibre of the contributors to it. Questions can attract a high proportion of uninformed and facile comments and need to be filtered carefully.

Online service providers

The internet can be accessed either through internet service providers (ISPs), of which there are many some national and some servicing local communities, or through online service providers. The latter (such as AOL, Compuserve (now merged) and Microsoft Network) are the best known and provide not only e-mail and access to the web but also direct access to their own forums and databases. Many of the online databases are designed for personal use and are of little use for research but some – such as the news services and company and financial databases – can be of considerable value.

The World Wide Web

The web (or www), introduced in 1994, is the vast network of individual sites accessible through the internet. They comprise sites established by governments, government agencies, research institutes, universities, trade associations, manufacturing companies, professional practices and even individuals. They contain data in the form of text, statistics, sound files and video images

Each web site has a unique address, or **uniform resource locator** (URL), by which it can be identified. The address, which is registered, contains the protocol, which permits the transfer of information from host to reader (normally http which stands for hypertext transfer protocol), the domain, the organisation whose site it is and the descriptor for the organisation (.com, .co, .org, .edu, .gov and .net depending on whether it is a company, non-profit organisation, educational organisation, government body or service provider).

The web has two major components:

- the **visible** web
- the **invisible** web.

The visible web is that which is written in HTML. This is the language used on the web which the search engines recognise. If sites are not written in HTML they will not be recognised by the search engines and are therefore invisible. Rewriting large numbers of pages in HTML is a time-consuming and costly activity which many site operators prefer not to do. If they wish to be visible, typically databases and government sites carrying large amounts of statistical information, they can provide an entry point to their site written in HTML. Others can be accessed only by registration, normally requiring fees to be paid. It is estimated that there are 500 million pages on the web of which 150 million pages are indexed by search engines and 350 million are unindexed.

The usefulness of the web for research is considerably enhanced by the fact that the flow of information can be two ways – from the publisher of the web site to the user and from the user to the site publisher. This means that web sites can not only be used to disseminate information but can also be used to **collect** information. The ability to incorporate a wide range of graphics and sound into web sites raises the potential of highly sophisticated data collection techniques which do not rely on the use of an interviewer or for the respondents to leave their homes or business premises.

12.3 **Advantages of the Internet for Research**

The reasons that researchers will be drawn inexorably towards the internet for survey research are that it has the potential to reduce research costs and speed up the data collection process whilst also improving research quality. The internet cannot, as yet, meet all research needs but it nevertheless offers researchers a number of advantages, some of which are unique.

Box 12.1 Research advantages of the Internet

In summary they are:

- Cost savings
- Low entry costs
- Global coverage
- Interactive
- Speed
- Access to sources
- Presentation
- Convenience.

Cost savings

Like the mail and the telephone the internet has the potential to reduce research costs. In internet research savings arise from the reduction or elimination of:

- time spent on library searches
- interviewer fees
- interviewer supervision costs
- printing or mailing costs
- data entry costs.

However, the internet is not a cost-free research medium. In order to carry out internet surveys professionally, investments need to be made in hardware and software. In addition, all surveys incur communications costs.

Although the investments can be amortised over a number of surveys, they offset some of the savings.

Low entry costs

Internet research can be carried out with minimal resources. Small organisations with sufficient computing power can search the net for data, send e-mail and internet questionnaires and analyse the findings. The requirement for access to field interviewing and supervisory resources is eliminated.

Global coverage

Internet connections are already global and as the number of connections increases the current bias towards the USA will diminish. International telephone surveys have long been a possibility but are relatively expensive due largely to the line charges and the need to employ multi-lingual interviewers. The expansion of the internet will make it possible to carry out international questionnaire-based surveys at substantially reduced costs.

Interactive

Internet questionnaires can be made interactive, thus combining some of the advantages of the traditional mail questionnaire with those of the telephone or personal interview.

Speed

Internet research can be significantly quicker than conventional survey research. Questionnaires can be set up and made available for simultaneous access by respondents world-wide, unencumbered by delays in the postal service or the time required by teams of interviewers to make contact. The questionnaires are returned in a form which is suitable for immediate data processing. Similarly, for secondary research the internet offers instant access to sites which can be downloaded for processing and incorporation into reports.

Access to Sources

In secondary research the internet has almost immeasurably broadened the range of sources that are available. Web sites cover considerably more territory than even the best stocked business libraries.

Presentation

Internet questionnaires can contain considerably more information than conventional approaches. They can be designed to incorporate pictures (still and moving) and sound as well as conventional text. This makes the internet an attractive possibility for research in which descriptive material needs to be shown before reactions can be taken, as in product tests and advertising research.

Convenience

Internet or e-mail questionnaires offer respondents the convenience of responding in their own time whereas telephone and personal interviewing can be intrusive. Interviewers calling during evening leisure time or during busy periods in the office are proving less and less welcome and are encountering higher incidences of answering machine and voice-mail responses. This problem can be circumvented to an extent by booking times for interviews but the internet or e-mail questionnaire could be a welcome and more interesting alternative.

12.4 Disadvantages of the Internet for Research

In the research context, the key disadvantages of the internet are:

- Inadequate samples
- Compatibility
- Verification of data
- Viruses.

Inadequate samples

The current structure of the user base of the internet means that it is difficult to obtain data from truly random or representative samples of respondents, unless the subject matter is intimately bound up with the internet itself or is on subjects which are relevant to respondent groups which have a high incidence of internet connections. Sampling companies – particularly large US companies – via the internet is likely to more successful than sampling individuals, purely because the incidence of corporate connections is already reasonably high.

However, the situation is changing rapidly. In the USA, where an estimated 24 per cent of households have access to a computer with an internet connection, research has shown that the differences between the online and offline populations are being eroded.[1]

Not surprisingly, a high proportion of the internet research carried out to date has been to test the use of the internet itself, to take reactions to web sites and to probe subjects which are of interest to IT professionals. It is also invaluable in probing the attitudes and requirements of those who are using the internet as a medium for shopping – or, to use the correct terminology, for **electronic commerce**. The growth of personal and business internet connections is being driven in part by the desire to use its commercial applications. This is advancing most rapidly in products which customers do not need to see prior to purchase, including books, flowers, music CDs, travel and entertainment bookings, but will gradually broaden to any item which is already being sold by mail order. Internet customers are automatically known to the supplier who is in an ideal position to interrogate them by means of an internet survey. By shortening the lines of communication between suppliers and customers and by eliminating intermediaries such as wholesalers and retailers, the internet is in a position to reshape markets and provide suppliers with the information they need to tailor their offers to the precise requirements of individual customers. In this sense, the use of the internet for research is an integral part of internet trading and will grow hand in hand with its use for commerce.

A secondary problem is that as with all research which relies on respondents to volunteer a response to a questionnaire, there is an inherent danger that the samples will be biased towards those individuals who have a particular reason for replying – commonly because they particularly dissatisfied or particularly satisfied with a product service or supplier.

The sampling problem can be overcome, but only at high cost. Sample households which participate in consumer panels, and are therefore committed to providing large quantities of information for a reasonable period of time, could be provided with the necessary equipment in order to transmit information to the research company. As equipment costs fall this option will become increasingly attractive as a means of speeding up the use of the internet as a sophisticated data capture mechanism.

Compatibility

Effective survey research on the internet demands not only that respondents have the required computer equipment and are broadly computer literate but also that the equipment is of adequate quality and speed to receive and display the images that are sent. It will be some time before electronic images are of the same quality as print but individual computers can compound the problem by having particularly poor displays. They may also be too slow, resulting in respondent boredom and a consequent unwillingness to download and complete questionnaires.

Verification of data

Secondary data obtained off the internet can come from any source and must be checked carefully before it is accepted. Whilst this is possible (as we shall show later) there are more serious problems with the verification of responses to internet questionnaires. These arise from the fact that, as with any research approach which does not involve the direct intervention of a researcher or interviewer, there is a loss of control. Multiple responses (the same individual replying many times in order to influence findings) and fictitious responses are already problem with internet surveys.

Viruses

The danger of importing viruses arises whenever computers are linked with the outside world and the internet is no exception. Warnings of particularly nasty viruses are circulated regularly between e-mail users but installing anti-virus software means that the real risk is extremely low. Nevertheless, some computer users are paranoid about viruses and this could reduce their enthusiasm to participate in internet research.

12.5 **Intranets**

The internal counterpart of the internet is the **intranet** which collects and disseminates data within organisations. As a replacement for the more traditional Management Information Systems, the intranet has a number of advantages. It is interactive, it can be linked with the outside 'Internet world', it is generally more user-friendly and it can reach all staff that have access to a PC. Intranets are becoming integral parts of corporate knowledge management systems through which information is collected, processed, stored and distributed. They can become the **central repository of all marketing information** and act as the link between those responsible for collecting information and those who use it, either in management or sales. The intranet can be the focus of the internal information auditing process and its presence can actively encourage staff to enter relevant information into the central database.

The interactive capabilities on the intranet make it a suitable vehicle for conducting surveys amongst staff to measure staff satisfaction and canvass staff opinions on management and management decisions.

12.6 **The Role for Internet Research**

Since the internet can meet only part of most data collection programmes, that which is 'Internet suitable' needs to be identified before any expenditure plans are made. Clearly the role of the internet will change from problem to problem but the following guidelines can be used to determine whether the internet represents an option as a data collection tool.

Secondary research

The internet is particularly valuable for secondary research and it should now be the starting point for all secondary information searches. Not everything is available on the internet, but given the speed at which secondary sources can be accessed, an internet search should be completed before more time-consuming library searches are carried out and more costly database searches attempted.

Although one of the advantages of the internet is that it can provide large amounts of information free of any charges other than telephone and connection fees, the internet and the online service providers will invariably lead to sites for which fees are payable and to avoid surprises it is essential to decide in advance how much can be spent on secondary data collection.

Business intelligence

Business intelligence relies on the ability to make contact with experts who can provide facts and informed opinions on markets. Traditionally, they are identified by contacting the companies, trade publications, trade associations, research organisations or universities in which they can be expected to be found and are interviewed in person or by telephone. The process is not necessarily laborious, but the canvas that can be covered in the time that is usually available is relatively limited – particularly in terms of geography.

The use of bulletin boards and discussion groups as a means of answering questions or providing opinions has become an established function of the internet and can be a useful mechanism for carrying out business intelligence – provided the credentials of those proffering information can be verified. The anonymity of the internet permits anyone to play the role of being an expert, and many do. Against this must be set the advantage of the global scale of the contacts that can be made through the internet and the broader range of expertise and opinion that can be accessed.

Survey research

The suitability of the internet for survey research is less certain and the following checklist of questions in Box 12.2 will help define whether it can be used at all – and, if so, the limits that must be placed on its use.

If the responses to those questions suggest than an unbiased sample of suitable respondents can be contacted through the internet, then an internet survey is feasible. If not, alternative research methods have to be identified.

In a situation in which the internet sample may be suitable but the degree of suitability is uncertain, it is possible to run a **split survey** – part using the internet and part using conventional techniques. A comparison of the results from the two components of the sample will show the level of consistency and the potential for using similar internet samples in future.

Box 12.2 Survey research on the internet

- Does the survey require respondents to be contacted in their place of work or their homes?
- What are the characteristics of the respondents that need to be contacted?
- What proportion of the universe is likely to have internet connections?
- Are there any reasons why those which have internet connections differ from those which do not (e.g. age group, income levels, occupations)?
- Can potential respondents be incentivised to respond to a questionnaire placed on a web site?
- Can the internet/e-mail addresses of potential respondents be obtained?
- How complete are those lists of addresses likely to be?
- Are the inclusions/exclusions from the list likely to be biased in any way?
- Is it feasible to provide internet connections for selected respondents that do not have them?

12.7 Using the Internet for Secondary Research

Although much of what is available on the net can also be accessed by other means, there is also data which is unique to the internet. The facility with which web sites can be created has encouraged many companies to put together portfolios of information about their activities which cannot be accessed by conventional searches. Furthermore, the fact that a search of world-wide sources can be carried out from the convenience of the office and is not constrained by the purchasing policies of the libraries provides the internet with a significant advantage in terms of convenience and coverage.

Searches on the internet have a labyrinthine quality that can puzzle the novice user but raises the chances that what is there will ultimately be found. Sites and services are linked either visibly or invisibly which means that following different avenues of enquiry can ultimately lead to the same destination. This means that persistence usually pays off, even if some wrong turns are taken during the search.

A wide range of data is available on the internet but that which is suitable for research purposes can be classified as follows. Those searching for company information are particularly well served, but there are a large number of sites providing data which meet the broader needs of business intelligence exercises:

- Country information
- Industry information
- Company information
- Technology and product information
- Market information
- News.

Country information

Information on countries is widely available on the internet in sources which range from the comprehensive *CIA Yearbook* to pages put up by various national and international organisations. The types of data that are available and relevant to market researchers include:

- Demographic information
- Education and literacy
- Healthcare
- Economic information
- National accounts
- Labour
- Foreign trade
- Forecasts
- Laws and regulations
- Political risk.

Industry information

Information on specific industries is also widely available in sources which include:

- Government statistics
- Non-governmental organisations (NGOs)
- Trade associations
- National and trade press
- Industry newsletters
- University sites
- Academic and business library sites.

A number of statistical authorities make data available on internet sites which include search facilities which improve the chances of finding the data being sought.

Company data

One of the great revelations of the internet is the volume of company data that can be accessed. The company data can be found in:

- Financial databases
- Company filings
- National and trade press articles
- Newsletters
- Company web sites
- Directory listings.

Company web sites are of particular interest for competitive intelligence since they can provide instant access to:

- company history and mission
- financial performance data
- lists of company facilities and the functions carried out in each one
- senior company personnel
- background information on the businesses in which the company is active
- product lists and product characteristics
- the text of press releases
- job vacancies.

Many companies have highly informative web sites which they see as an opportunity to showcase their activities.

Technology and product information

The trade and technical press and industry newsletters provide a wealth of technical information and many of them can be accessed either on the web or through the online service providers.

Market information

An increasing number of publishers of market reports are using the internet as a means of distributing their data. Publishers' web sites provide a list of the reports that are available and either an order form or a means of accessing the reports online. There are signs that the web will become a serious rival to the operators of online databases as report publishers find that direct access to the market for their data is a more lucrative option and preferable in the sense that they can make direct contact with the report users.

News

One method of keeping abreast of company, industry and market information is to scan the news as it evolves. For some businesses this is a task which can be carried out by scanning the national dailies and the relevant trade press. As businesses become larger and more complex the magnitude of the task escalates and takes increasing amounts of time. The internet offers a growing number of facilities for searching for relevant news stories and feeding them directly to the researcher via the internet. Relevance is established by setting criteria which are used to screen articles. The process is automatic and reasonably comprehensive.[2]

12.8 **Searching the Web for Data**

Although there are hard copy (*Yellow Page*) directories of web sites, the most common and most effective method of identifying information that is available is to use a **search engine** (see below). Directory publishers have to be selective and even then have a hard time keeping pace with new sites. The search engines will identify sites that are there, provided they are written in a language they understand. Unfortunately, the size of even the visible web defeats the most powerful search engines and they connect with only a small proportion of sites specified in the search. The main problem is the rate at which the web is growing and the amount of change that is occurring, which makes it virtually impossible to index the entire web and keep the index up to date. The problem is being solved to a limited extent by the emergence of intermediaries who create composite sites which bring together data on specific topics and embody hyperlinks to the original sites. For example, *www.ResearchInfo.com* provides a service to users of market research services and market researchers. It contains:

- **Market Research Chat** – a forum on market research containing a message board and Live-chat
- **Research Company Directory** – a listing of market research companies
- **Peer Poll** – offering the facility to vote on topics related to market research and see how the user's opinion compares with that of others
- **Employment Board** – providing a job-finding function
- **Market Research Library** – articles on research topics submitted by research professionals
- **Legislative Watch** – providing information on legislative issues which affect the research business
- **Web Survey Tutorial** – instructions on how to create online survey content
- **E-Mail Directory** – to find contacts in the research business
- **Market Research Calculators** – a selection of statistical tools for researchers.

Search engines

Although far from perfect, search engines are fundamental to getting good results on the internet. Researchers have a number of engines which can be used, each of which has its strengths and weaknesses. An unproductive search with one engine does not mean that data is unavailable since changing engines can frequently reveal further information. The main alternatives are:

- Yahoo (http://www.yahoo.com)
- AltaVista (http://www.altavista.digital.com)
- Infoseek (http://www.infoseek.com)

- Excite (http://www.excite.com)
- Lycos (http://www.lycos.com)
- MetaCrawler (http://www.metacrawler.com).

Search engines are free of charge to users because they are paid for by advertising material. The advertising can be intrusive in the sense that opening pages are cluttered and the graphics take time to download, but it is otherwise harmless. All search engines work on the principle of identifying sites which (apparently) meet the criteria inserted by users. The sites can be opened by clicking on the text.

Yahoo
Yahoo is the internet equivalent of *Yellow Pages*. It is a *library* of sites that have been registered with it and funnels searchers towards their objectives either through a hierarchy of categories shown on the title pages or by searching on key words. To identify market research companies using the hierarchy of categories the user would need to click successively on **marketing, companies** and **market research**. Alternatively **market + research** can be inserted in the text box. The latter approach will generally produce a large number of records since every site containing the words 'market' and 'research' will be identified.

AltaVista
AltaVista covers more ground than Yahoo by indexing the contents of 35 million web sites. Searches are carried out by inserting key words in dialogue boxes and by a function which permits the searcher to narrow down the search criteria so that extraneous sites are eliminated.

Infoseek
Infoseek indexes almost twice the number of sites as AltaVista and is interesting to researchers in that it is easier to refine the search before the site names are called up. It works through a hierarchy which (using the example quoted above) enables the searcher to identify all sites covering market and research (**market|research**) then search within the sites thus identified to locate companies and go on to **UK, internet** or whatever. Eventually the number of sites identified will be whittled down to a small number which meet a very highly refined set of search criteria.

Excite
Excite covers territory which is as broad as Infoseek and is the only search engine which permits Boolean enquiries. It also contains an editorial function which indicates the quality of the site before it is opened. It also has a **'more like this'** function which enables searchers to identify other sites which have similar characteristics to a particular site they have identified.

Other services offered by Excite which are potentially useful are an address and telephone number finder for individuals in the USA, an e-mail lookup to find internet addresses and 'Yellow Pages' for business addresses.

Lycos
A similar engine to Excite offering e-mail services, directories and links to information on specific topics.

MetaCrawler
MetaCrawler uses the resources six of the main search engines to identify sites meeting search criteria. Duplicates are eliminated and the time taken to complete the search process can be reduced.

12.9 Limits of the Internet for Secondary Research

The main problems with the internet as an information source arise almost entirely from its size and the rate at which it is growing. With 500 million pages of data already accessible and 50,000 new domains being added per month, it should not be surprising that access is a problem. The second problem is verifying that the data recovered is accurate.

12.10 Features of the Internet which Improve Secondary Research Efficiency

Given the scale of the internet, it is not particularly helpful to reinvent the wheel on each search. Some sites take time and ingenuity to locate and if they are likely to be of lasting interest – commonly the case for researchers working in specific business sectors – it is important to note their location. This can be done manually but regular searchers on the internet can make use of the facility to **bookmark** sites which are particularly useful and to set up **site monitors** which provide alerts when changes are made or new information is available.

Bookmarking

Bookmarks enable the internet user to return to sites that have been found to be useful. All browsers offer the facility to store references to useful sites in a list of 'favourites'. Whenever the user clicks on the **favourites** button on the toolbar the list of sites which have been bookmarked will appear. Re-entering sites can be achieved by clicking on the site name. Within the 'favourites' facility it is usually possible to create folders in which sites can be grouped. It is therefore possible to set up a system of folders such as:

- Statistics
- News
- Trade journals
- Technology
- Competitors

in which sites relevant to each topic can be bookmarked. This process eliminates the need to remember sites that are worth following and automates the process of returning to them.

Subscribing to sites

Subscribing to sites is a process which directs the computer to download sites at regular intervals and store them on the hard disk where they can be browsed offline. It also notifies the user whenever a site has been changed thus providing an alert to the fact that new information may be available. This process is particularly valuable for tracking competitors' web sites or others where there are likely to be additions at irregular intervals.

12.11 Verification of Information Downloaded from the Internet

Verification of the information available from internet sites is essential. There is no control over what is placed on the internet and although a high proportion of what can be accessed is accurate and useful there is also a considerable amount of rubbish. The openness of the internet means that it attracts a large number of cranks who use it as a low-cost way of seeing their name in print. This means that researchers using the internet need to develop a mechanism for checking the quality of the information they have identified (Box 12.3).[3]

Box 12.3 Internet data verification

The basic checks that should be carried out are much the same as those that would be used to verify any published data and include:

- author
- publisher
- web site
- date

- purpose
- methodology
- cross-checks.

Author

As with any published data the identity of the author, be it an individual, or an organisation, is the primary indicator of authenticity and accuracy. The easiest to check are known names whose other work can be read. Prolific publishers, such as major research companies, are likely to have a reputation which can be checked by reference to other users. The fact that an author is unknown does not make the work inaccurate but does mean that the verification process is more complex. The signals of authenticity are:

- the provision of **complete provenance and contact details** on the author; a desire for anonymity is a sign of potential problems
- **references to the author in other documents** suggests that others have used the work and found it to be accurate
- **biographical details and experience statements**, which permit the reader to judge the level of authority from which the author is writing
- attribution of data that has been extracted from **other secondary sources** is an indication that the author takes the research process seriously.

Publisher

If the publisher of the data is different to the author, the publishers' identity can help authenticate the data. As with authors, known publishers with an established track record and a reputation for quality are more trustworthy than unknown publishers. If the publisher is unknown, the availability of information on who they are and how they can be located provides an opportunity to check up on them either directly or by seeking information from others that may have used their data.

Web site

The ease with which anyone can put up a web site on a host system has already been demonstrated. Use of a host does not indicate poor quality but publishers who run their own server are easier to check up on. It is also likely that personal web pages are more dubious in quality than organisational pages. Documents which are 'self-published' have always been more suspect than those that have gone through the hands of a recognised publisher.

Publication date

As with any information, the date the information was published shows its currency. Statistics are usually (though not always) tied to specific dates but technical information and company data loses value as it ages. Users should therefore check that the publication date is included in the documents, usually in the form 'site last updated. . .'.

Purpose

It is useful to establish the reason the site has been established. Government and international organisation sites which set out to provide factual information are likely to be reasonably accurate. However, there could be a significant difference in objectivity between a site put up by a government statistical service which is designed only to inform, and one put up by a government tourist authority which is designed to attract visitors. Company web sites have an obvious promotional purpose which means that although it unlikely that the data they contain will be knowingly inaccurate, it may be slanted to place the corporation in the most favourable light. If the purpose of putting up a site is to peddle a particular political or social point of view or support a particular cause, there is a possibility that the data will be at worst biased and at best selective.

Methodology

The provision of details on how the data on a web site has been collected is another primary indication of quality and authenticity. Data which has been collected by techniques which are fully described have more credibility than a set of facts or statements whose origins are completely unknown.

Cross-checks

The ultimate test of authenticity is whether the data cross-checks with similar data obtained from other sites and other sources. Similar data sets arising from a number of independent sources suggests accuracy, though it is always possible that inaccurate data emanating from a single source is being picked up and broadcast by a number of independent publishers. This is common in the newspaper world where different journals pick up and publish the same press release without checking its accuracy. Remember that facts gain in stature the more frequently they are published, regardless of their accuracy.

12.12 Locating Forums, Bulletin Boards and Discussion Groups

Forums, bulletin boards and discussion groups can play a number of roles in internet research and are a unique benefit that the internet has created for researchers. However, to use them they must first be identified and tested to ensure that they are relevant. This is not difficult. Even though there are some 20,000 internet forums listed on Usenet and a further 10,000 on the average service provider they are reasonably well indexed and can be located by:

- the service provider
- the search engines
- internet sites such as Deja News (http://www.dejanews.com).

The service provider

Online service providers provide access to discussion forums and newsgroups directly from their title pages. Access to the forum listings is either direct or through the special topic listings. Forums are indexed by topic and then, within the topic, by specific subject.

The search engines

Excite offers the facility to search Usenet discussion groups on the internet. General topic listings provide the first level of entry and this is followed by listing of specific forums.

Specific internet sites

Deja News searches Usenet in much the same way as Excite but rather than following a hierarchy of subjects enables the user to enter a topic and execute a search for suitable sites.

Subscribing to forums

Subscribing to a discussion forum is identical to subscribing to an internet site by adding it to the 'favourites' list. The function is normally carried out within the **Tools** header which offers the opportunity to **Subscribe**.

Verification of forums

It goes without saying that a forum is only as useful as its members. The only way to establish the quality of the membership is to make trial use of the group. As with all other aspects of the internet, there is ample opportunity for interventions by individuals who are unqualified to comment but usage will soon show whether the participants are providing sound comment.

12.13 Using the Internet for Survey Research

As a method of communication with respondents the internet is in much the same position now as the telephone was 20–30 years ago. Compared with the more time-consuming personal interviews the telephone offered the advantages of speed, national coverage and a novel and 'imperative' approach which would gain access to respondents. The main disadvantage of the telephone was that although business penetration was soon close to 100 per cent, residential penetration was not and it was therefore difficult to draw representative samples. However, the promise was there and researchers could see that as telephone ownership increased it would become an extremely valuable research tool.

Much the same is true of the internet today. With internet penetration of households at less than 2 per cent it is far from suitable for general survey work. For business surveys the situation is considerably better but although penetration rates are increasing rapidly they too are still insufficient for widespread business surveys. However, overall penetration rates disguise substantial variations in the proportion of specific population groups that are connected. Although there are many groups in which internet connections are negligible or non-existent, such as low-income groups and the elderly, there are others in which the penetration is high, such as home computer users and IT companies, multinationals and other large organisations. For the period during which internet penetration is increasing its use for survey research will be restricted to those population groups in which the number of internet connections are high. Not surprisingly, much of the initial survey research on the internet has been about internet users.

Internet research can be carried out either by e-mail or by respondents logging on to web sites to download a questionnaire for completion. Specialist software has been developed for both routes and exploits the possibility not only of collecting information quickly but also to modify the line of questioning in the light of responses given.

E-mail or internet questionnaires

The first decision is whether the survey is to be carried out by e-mail questionnaires or by a questionnaire placed on a web site. E-mail has the advantage of being simple to activate. The questionnaire can be designed in a word processing package and sent as an attachment to a covering letter. E-mail can also be targeted to specific respondents for whom e-mail addresses have been acquired.

The main disadvantages are that an e-mail questionnaire is a **static document**, comparable to a questionnaire sent through the post, and cannot be made interactive or dynamic. Furthermore once an e-mail questionnaire has been returned the data has to be transcribed from the e-mail into an analysis package. Software exists to automate this process, but a high proportion of researchers use conventional data entry techniques with which they are familiar.

Although messages do get lost and fail to be delivered, e-mail facilities generally work well, especially when messages are being transferred between users of the same service provider. From a respondent standpoint the problems that are encountered with e-mail can be the time taken to download complex questionnaires, particularly if they contain images, and the amount of storage space they take up. These problems are most acute for owners of older PCs and slow modems but will gradually disappear as the average speed of the installed base of equipment rises.

Questionnaires to be placed on web sites are complex to write and require a high level of skill in the chosen language. Their main advantage over e-mail is the level of sophistication that can be introduced including interactivity, skip patterns and verification routines. The application of internet questionnaires is complicated by the fact that they require an additional mechanism to:

• entice suitable respondents to enter the web site and provide responses
• eliminate responses from those who enter the site inadvertently and respond regardless of the fact that they have not been invited.

Questionnaires on web sites can either be open to all respondents that find them or answered by those to whom invitations have been issued by e-mail or by telephone, the latter adding an element of control and persuasion but adding cost.

Internet questionnaires pay off in the analysis stage, which is completely automated, particularly when the number of responses that is being sought is high.

Sampling

The limits on the coverage of an internet sample have already been referred to.[4] Clearly whether the internet is used depends on whether a representative sample can be contacted. The mechanisms for identifying and building samples of potential respondents lie within the internet itself and include:

• e-mail directories
• forums and bulletin boards
• company web sites
• internet advertisements
• web panels.

E-mail directories
A number of general e-mail directories exist on the internet. The largest are

• Big Foot (http://www.bigfoot.com)
• Four 11 (http://www.four11.com)
• Infospace (http://www.infospace.com)
• Internet Address Finder (http://www.iaf.com)

- Switchboard (http://switchboard.com)
- WhoWhere (http://whowhere.com)
- Yelloweb Europe (http://yweb.com)

These can have 6–7 million entries each and comprise both 'White' and 'Yellow Pages'. They can be accessed directly, through the Excite and Lycos search engines which offer a connection, or through http://www.555-1212.com. Addresses are also provided by the directory services of the internet service providers – which list all of their own subscribers. The main problem with the internet directories is that they are very far from comprehensive. Unless a subscriber has registered with a service, the name is unlikely to be listed The service provider listings should be comprehensive and up to date but to sample from the total universe it would be necessary to access the directories of all service providers. This is logistically difficult though not impossible – certainly within a specific country. Finally there are hundreds of special interest sites which contain lists of e-mail addresses as part of their content. These can be invaluable when they correspond with the subject matter of the survey.

Forums and bulletin boards
Forums and bulletin boards offer an alternative mechanism for identifying potential respondents with special interests. The main problem is that respondents identified this way are a self-selected sample and the responses they provide must therefore be treated with considerable caution. Furthermore, the use of a sample identification technique which is open for all to observe gives rise to the concern that a campaign could be organised to stimulate responses from members of pressure groups with a specific message to convey or lead to disproportionate responses from particular types of respondent. If it happened, this would certainly compromise the integrity of the survey findings.

Company web sites
Company web sites commonly provide e-mail/internet addresses. Although these may identify particular individuals within the company they are more likely to be a general access point and therefore unsuitable for research purposes.
Web sites can also be used as a mechanism for signing up visitors to the site as potential respondents for surveys being carried out by the site owner. This has the advantage of ensuring that the sample has an interest in the topic covered by the site, often difficult to achieve by other techniques, other than by an expensive screening process.

Internet advertisements
Respondents can be recruited to respond to internet surveys by placing advertisements at suitable points such as the browsers or on pages which are

related to the subject matter of the survey. For a travel survey a questionnaire could be advertised on travel and airline booking pages. Advertising on the internet is costly and would be justified only for a large-scale survey, but the most significant problems are those created by the loss of control over who replies and the risk of deliberate or inadvertent bias.

Web panels

A number of research companies have created panels of respondents who can be accessed for research purposes via the internet. The panels are recruited by advertising on the internet – usually the research company's own web site. Potential panel members are asked to complete a questionnaire which establishes their demographic characteristics and their interests. Applicants can be rejected if they are unsuitable or if the panel is already fully loaded with its quota of respondents. Once accepted, respondents become eligible to participate in online, e-mail surveys or focus groups. They may also be invited to participate in conventional surveys. Panel members are paid an incentive to participate in surveys and may also participate in prize draws.

The main advantage of web panels is that although they are bound by the limits imposed by PC ownership and internet access, sampling can be more strictly controlled for each survey and response rates are likely to be sufficiently high to reduce the element of bias caused by non-response.

12.14 Internet Questionnaires

The web provides an alternative method of 'distributing' questionnaires and collecting responses. Many web sites incorporate a simple questionnaire, or registration form, designed to collect information from visitors to the site. The data usually covers the name and address of the visitor plus telephone and fax numbers, e-mail address and any comments about the site that the visitor wishes to make – research at its simplest. The provision of the data may be made a condition for visiting the site, in which case it becomes an active, as opposed to a passive, mechanism for collecting data on individuals and organisations with an interest in the site operator.

For more complex data collection, the internet can be used as means of distributing questionnaires either by e-mail or though a web site. E-Mail questionnaires are identical in format to paper questionnaires but distributed electronically. They can be sent either as an e-mail message or as an attachment. Depending on the software, there may be limits on the size of a questionnaire sent as an e-mail message, though if this was the case the questionnaire is probably too long. There is no restriction on the size of questionnaires sent as attachments but their main advantage is that they can be formatted more attractively and can contain graphics which may encourage higher levels of response. The danger of attachments is that not all respondents may be able to download them or read them.

Web questionnaires are written in HTML and are posted on a web site where they can be accessed by respondents who have been alerted to their existence (commonly by e-mail) and motivated to respond. They have all the features of conventional questionnaires and some of those of CASI questionnaires. The questionnaires can incorporate questions which invite multiple, single and open-ended responses, skip patterns which navigate respondents through the questionnaire according to the responses given and radio buttons, data entry fields and edit checks which prevent impossible choices. The graphics facilities are superior to e-mail, in that they can include animation or full video, and web questionnaires can also incorporate sound.

Designing an e-mail or internet questionnaire is no different in principle to a paper questionnaire or one which is to be administered by computer. Indeed it is important that the principles of good questionnaire design are incorporated into internet questionnaires. These include the ability to rotate questions to avoid ordering effects, the introduction of skip patterns and the checking of responses for consistency. However, there are some additional factors which need to be considered to encourage response and to ensure that respondents complete all questionnaires. These are:

- explanations
- brevity
- format
- design
- enticement
- avoiding 'spamming'.

Explanations

All questionnaires should contain an introductory statement explaining the purpose of the survey, the identity of the sponsor (if this can be revealed), the use that will be made of the data, a promise of anonymity, the number of questions in the questionnaire and the amount of time required to complete the questionnaire.

Brevity

The first rule is that questionnaires should be short and as simple as possible. As with questionnaires sent by mail, long questionnaires with complex questions look intimidating and will discourage respondents from cooperating. The absence of an interviewer to encourage responses means that the questionnaire has to provide all the encouragement itself. The ability to incorporate graphics can help prolong respondents' attention span but not indefinitely. In addition to being quick to respond to, the questionnaire should also be quick to access.

Format

Structured questions, to which the respondents need only choose responses from options presented to them, are preferable to open ended questions, to which replies are given in the respondents' own words. Structured questions are quicker to respond to, they are easier to analyse and they do not demand any keyboard skills from the respondents. Typing several sentences of script can be a discouragement to respond.

Design

The questionnaire design must recognise that a screen display is not always easy to read, even by those who do not suffer from eye problems. Small, difficult to read fonts, bright colours, garish graphics and devices such as flashing lights and displays can all discourage respondents or cause them to break off before completing the questionnaire. The questionnaire should also avoid items which take time to download. Respondents required to wait several minutes whilst complex graphics are downloaded may become impatient and switch off.

Enticement

Some form of encouragement to respond should always be given serious consideration. This may take the form of a gift dispatched to all survey participants, entry into a prize draw or a donation to charity.

Avoiding 'spamming'

'Spamming' is the use of the internet to broadcast unsolicited advertising messages. It is unpopular with recipients and is illegal in some countries. The lists that are created as a result of respondents participating in a survey must remain confidential. If there is any suggestion that respondents are 'spammed' as a consequence of participating in an e-mail or internet survey, hostility will soon build up to the point where response rates will become too low to be useful.

12.15 **Preparing the Internet Questionnaire**

Writing an internet questionnaire requires skills which are normally beyond that of the average researcher and research user and requires the services of someone familiar with the HTML language. Although simple web authoring and publishing tools to compose web pages are widely available, the level of sophistication required for a questionnaire which incorporates several research devices is considerably higher. Companies that do not have their own programming staff can overcome the problem by using one of the numerous service bureau that have been established.

12.16 **Internet focus groups**

Group discussions on the internet are being offered in the USA at costs which compare very favourably with the conventional version of the technique. They can be carried out in two ways:

- online
- offline.

Online discussions

Online discussions require a sample of respondents to log onto a site simultaneously at an agreed time. They then respond to questions keyed in by the moderator by typing their responses. Transcripts of the discussion are available within minutes of the discussion being completed, thereby speeding up the analysis process considerably and making them ideally suited for research programmes which have to be completed quickly.

Offline discussions

Offline discussions can be carried out using special interest discussion groups and bulletin boards which proliferate on the internet. Questions put to discussion groups produce a round of responses which can be recycled, either with specific individuals that have responded or with the group at large, until enough opinions have been collected. The process is slower than online groups but is potentially richer in that a much broader range of responses can be collected and the respondents themselves tend to be highly informed. The limits to the offline approach are the availability of a suitable discussion group and the fact that questions and answers tend to be relatively short

The internet group offers many of the advantages of a conventional group discussion without the disadvantages of lengthy set-up time and the need to travel to a group discussion facility. Internet group discussions cannot be observed and the rate at which they can be completed and the fullness of the responses depends heavily on the keyboard skills of the respondents. Nevertheless, they appear to represent an interesting addition to the research armoury particularly if quick qualitative studies are required and there is an advantage in being able to include respondents living in areas remote from established group discussion facilities.

12.17 **Internet Depth Interviews**

One-on-one depth interviews on the internet are feasible and have been used to a limited extent. The interviewer and the respondent are connected online and the latter responds to the former by typing responses to questions. As with the online focus groups, internet interviews are quick and the transcripts are available immediately. The technique requires reasonable keyboard skills to be successful and financial compensation is necessary since the respondent pays for telephone connect time.

12.18 **Pilot Survey**

As with any research technique it is essential to pilot an e-mail or internet questionnaire before launching the full survey. The pilot survey will be used to test the acceptability of the questionnaire, the existence of questions which are ambiguous or poorly worded, whether the questionnaire will be completed fully, the ability of respondents to answer the questions, the willingness of respondents to answer the questions and the apparent quality of the responses. E-mail surveys can be tested by sending them to a pilot sample of respondents, in which case a preliminary indication of the response rate is also obtained. Internet questionnaires need to be handled more carefully. If respondents are being invited to respond, the web site can be created and a small sample of invitations issued. If the responses are to be generated by some form of promotion of the site, it is preferable to carry out the pilot offline with respondents recruited to test the questionnaire.

12.19 **Testing for the Effects of Non-response**

The normal level of response to internet surveys has yet to be established but where response rates are less than 100 per cent there is a possibility that the findings are biased by the fact that the respondents are not truly representative of the universe sampled. This risk increases as the response rate falls. The risk is further compounded in internet surveys by the inherent biases which can exist in the characteristics of the individuals that have internet connections. This means that the results of the survey carried out on the internet must be checked to verify that the characteristics of those individuals that have responded are identical to those that did not.

Where the survey has been aimed at a predetermined sample of respondents and the non-responders can therefore be identified, verification can be carried out by resampling from the group that did not respond and checking that the results from this control group are similar to those from the group that replied in the first round. With internet surveys for which there is no prior identification of respondents the verification process is more difficult, but equally essential. The most reliable verification technique is to run a **control sample** using a conventional research approach such as telephone interviews, and compare the findings with those obtained from the internet. 10–20 per cent of the total questionnaires should allocated to conventional interview methods in order to provide adequate control of the findings. This obviously increases the cost but avoids the pitfalls of a totally electronic approach.

Notes

1 Statement by Charles Hamlin, President of Interactive/High Technology and Telecommunications research at NFO Worldwide Inc.
2 One example of such a service is ClariNews provided by ClariNet Communications Corporation. The service scans all the major sources of real time news.
3 For further information see the writings of Elizabeth E. Kirk to be found through the ResearchInfo.com internet site.
4 A survey of the number and characteristics of internet connections is carried out regularly by the Graphics, Visualisation and Usability (GVU) Centre at the Georgia Institute of Technology. Their WWW User Surveys are published on the internet at www.gvu.gatech.edu/user-survey.

13 The Research Mix

In research there are many ways of reaching the same objective. The difference between a survey approach and a business intelligence approach has already been referred to but even within each of those the mix of techniques can be variously structured to suit the objectives, the market environment and the budget that is available. In the ideal world of the academic researcher the research mix is driven by technical research considerations. In the real business world the enthusiasm for technique is invariably tempered by practical considerations such as cost and time.

The key factors which determine the mix of data collection techniques to be used in a survey are given in Box 13.1.

Box 13.1 Data collection techniques: the best mix

- Budget availability
- Time that is available to complete the research programme
- Type of data that is required
- Availability of data from secondary sources
- Volume and complexity of the data required from each respondent
- Sources of data
- Expected response rates
- Accuracy levels required
- Geographical scope of research programme
- Research resources that are available.

All of these can affect the approach that is adopted but in some situations a single factor can override all others and in effect dictate the way in which the data is collected. Consideration of each of them in turn will show the flow of decisions which lead to the ultimate choice of research approach.

13.1 The Budget

The starting point for all research decisions is the **budget that is available**. Large and complex research programmes can cost significant sums and if these are not available then the research process must be simplified and orientated towards low-cost techniques.

In many companies which are established and regular users of research a research budget is set at the beginning of each year based on known commitments, historical experience and expectations of research activities that will be required during the budget period. The large-scale users of research typically include manufacturers of all types of consumer products, providers of financial services, pharmaceutical companies, telecommunications companies, suppliers of information technology equipment and software, retailers and airlines. The common denominator for all of these organisations is that they operate in large and complex markets in which there is fierce competition for market share and which require the use of the full battery of marketing techniques. They also operate in an environment where the cost of new product development is high. Traditionally there has always been a strong correlation between advertising expenditure and expenditure on market research. This is partly because the need for heavy advertising stems from the same imperatives which create the need for market research. However, the relationship is also established by the fact that advertising plans need research data, and the planners within advertising agencies are constantly requesting their clients to invest in research.

Heavy research users whose annual requirements are known in advance and can be budgeted for are the exception rather than the rule. They are vastly outweighed by medium and light research users whose requirements are spasmodic and who in many cases never get as far as establishing a formal research budget. In these organisations the budget is set as and when required for individual projects and may be taken out of some general marketing or contingency fund. In this situation – and indeed within the major research users when they confront an unforeseen research problem – there is a need to establish what funds can be made available for each specific piece of research.

Budgeting decisions must commence with the value that is placed on the data. For all research users the key question is not 'how much does the research cost' but **what is the data worth**? All information has a value to the user and the cost of the research required to obtain it can be justified only if it is equal to or lower than the value that will be gained from its use. In any situation in which the cost of acquiring the information is higher than its value it must be admitted that the research may not be worth carrying out. Unfortunately, whereas the cost of research is clear and highly tangible, its value is much harder to quantify. The value of market data is determined by its ability to ensure that correct decisions are taken and that business risk is minimised. Just occasionally the value is obvious, as in a competitive pricing study which enables the research user to increase prices and still remain competitive, but normally research data is only one of a number of inputs which contribute to successful decisions, and its impact may be impossible to isolate.

Regular research users are better equipped through experience to assess value. Data is part of their daily decision making process and experience tells them how disadvantaged they would be without it. In most other situations there is a bias against using research mainly because users are unwilling to risk funds on an activity that may not yield a direct benefit. The investment is much easier to assess after the data has been obtained and used, especially if the research users can see that without it they would probably have made the wrong decisions – but to get that far requires an act of faith. It is usually easier for research users to appreciate the value of data when they are confronting completely new situations outside their previous business experience. Wherever some level of market knowledge or experience exists it is far easier to be convinced that research is an expensive luxury.

There is therefore a significant difference between what marketing teams **should** invest in research and that which they **actually do** invest. What they should invest is determined by a series of considerations which include:

- the scale of the investment that is planned
- the levels of additional sales and profits that could be made from the investment
- what is at risk if a wrong decision is taken
- the level of supporting information that will be required by senior management, owners and external investors
- the cost of alternative methods of arriving at a conclusion.

Big investment, high risk, major need to convince managers or investors that the risk is worth taking and no alternative methods of acquiring the data all point in the direction of a significant need for research. However, there are no rigid guidelines and the size of the actual research budget generally depends on:

- the funds that are available
- the individual attitudes, approaches and experience of the managers concerned
- the size of the organisation making the decision.

However strong the case for a research programme the company may not have the cash available to pay for it. Start-up companies are highly vulnerable organisations whose knowledge of the markets they are seeking to enter is often minimal. Nevertheless, in a straight choice between a market survey or a refinement of their production process which will improve product quality or reduce costs, the investment in production will invariably win. Unless some outside organisation, such as the venture capital fund providing the finance, insists that research is done.

Personalities also play a significant role in determining whether research is used. Those who are risk averse are more likely to require the support of research data before taking decisions than those who are comfortable operating in risky environments. Marketing management that has risen up through the ranks of the sales team is less likely to appreciate the value of independently obtained data than those that have come up through the product management and business development routes. Sharp-end experience with customers or distributors provides in-depth knowledge of a marketplace and those that have acquired it are reluctant to concede that what they see as an academic research programme can contribute much more than they know already – and researchers need to be prepared to acknowledge that they might be right.

Large corporations, where decisions are made by professional managers, tend to be more prolific users of research than small entrepreneurial, owner-managed companies. Large companies are also more likely to be taking decisions on bigger and riskier projects and to have the funds available for marketing research, but their management is also more remote from customers and the daily activities in the marketplace.

Alternatives to research must always be considered. For small-scale decisions, trial and error may prove a better and lower-cost approach than a market survey. For example, simple product modifications can be implemented and tried on customers to test their effect rather than use complex research procedures. The effectiveness of new distribution channels can also be tested by trial rather than research

13.2 Time

The **time available to complete the research programme** is the second major determinant of the research mix. When time is available the research can be large-scale and can make use of time-consuming techniques. Where time is not available the research user will be driven towards readily available data such as syndicated or secondary research, or if this does not meet the need, a short business intelligence exercise might be commissioned. Time constraints also suggest the use of techniques which can be applied quickly but with no loss of coverage. Thus a telephone approach may be favoured over personal interviews purely because it can be mounted and completed quickly.

Time is a commodity which is just as valuable as cash and whereas in an ideal world the business or market planning process should take as much time as is required to complete it properly, there are many situations where adequate amounts of time are simply not available. The product launch which needs to meet a deadline set by competitor activity, the evaluation of a market prior to deciding whether to take up a licence which is on offer for a limited period, the assessment of a marketing situation which has gone seriously wrong for a supplier who is as a result haemorrhaging sales to competition are all examples of situations in which time will constrain what can be done. In other situations impatience and the need to make progress quickly can also act as a spur to the research process. Less seriously – though no less effective in hastening research action – events such as the approach of the year end and the need to dispose of research budget (for fear that if not spent it might be lost in the following year) can also initiate a requirement for a quickly executed research programme.

13.3 The Type of Data Required

When budgets and time are not constraints the types of research data required will normally be the main determinant of the mix of techniques. Qualitative data must be derived from techniques which permit in-depth probing of respondents' attitudes and requirements which means the use of group discussions and in-depth personal interviews. Quantitative research requires the use of techniques which are appropriate for large-scale survey approaches. This normally implies structured street or household interviews and, increasingly commonly, telephone surveys, e-mail and internet questionnaires.

13.4 Availability of Data from Secondary Sources

The **value of secondary data** is a lesson which the survey researcher needs to learn from the business intelligence specialist. The latter have always recognised the contribution that secondary sources can make whereas the former have tended to ignore them except as a potential method of validating the data derived from surveys. However, nobody should want to pay for data which has already been collected and can be accessed from secondary sources. The widespread association of market research with field surveys designed to collect primary data needs to be dispelled and replaced by a realisation that an effective search of secondary sources may provide a solution in itself, or may at least lead to the more efficient use of primary data collection techniques.

The reluctance to carry out a secondary data search stems either from ignorance of what can be achieved or from previous unfruitful experiences. It has to be admitted that whilst there are many situations in which secondary data can make a valuable contribution to the information requirement there are many more in which secondary sources are useless. The problem is compounded by the fact that the value of secondary sources can rarely be established without actually consulting them and it is entirely possible that a lengthy search will yield no useful data. It is also the case that secondary sources are gradually becoming more valuable and more accessible, largely because of the growth of the online databases and the internet as mechanisms for accessing established sources and for locating new sources.

What is available from secondary sources may lead to more targeted uses of primary data collection techniques – permitting them to concentrate on issues which can be covered only by primary research. This could result in a more sparing use of primary research or a concentration on techniques which explain rather than quantify.

13.5 The Volume and Complexity of the Data Required

Surveys which require substantial volumes of data from respondents or data which is complex will tend to depend on a personal approach, place and collect questionnaires or diaries which permit the collection of data over time. The more superficial approaches, such as telephone interviews, are suited only to the collection of information which respondents can provide instantly and do not require lengthy consideration, checking of records or continuous recording.

13.6 Sources of Data

The characteristics of the individuals that are to be used as information sources must be taken into account when selecting the research method. The factors to be considered are:

- where can they be **located**
- how difficult will they be to **identify**
- how much time will they be **prepared to devote** to the survey
- what needs to be done to **encourage them to participate**.

The most straightforward surveys are those for which the qualification criteria for respondents are minimal and where they can be located at home, on the high street or in offices and other places of work. As the qualifications for eligibility become more stringent – such as ownership of a particular item, participating in a particular activity or fulfilling a particular job function – respondents become more difficult to locate and the research method needs to change accordingly. This may be as simple as including screening questions on the questionnaire or siting interviews at points where qualifying individuals are certain to congregate (at airports for air travellers, outside computer outlets for owners of PCs). Alternatively it may require a separate research activity devoted entirely to the identification of individuals who qualify. For example samples of minority groups can be located by acquiring the subscription lists of journals they are likely to read or by placing questions on omnibus surveys.

Some types of respondents are not inherently difficult to identify but they are difficult either to locate or to persuade to cooperate. Salespeople, farmers, builders, plumbers and maintenance staff who are continuously mobile are notoriously difficult to make contact with. Senior management may be less mobile but more reluctant to allocate precious working time to an interview. A common solution is to interview them in the evenings at their home but, assuming their home addresses are available, this means that the interview takes place at a time when they are tired and trying to relax and, if they do agree to cooperate, are tempted to give hurried responses. An alternative approach is to make an appointment to interview them at a time to suit their work schedule. This requires the use of an appointment booking routine to supplement the interview programme itself.

13.7 **Expected Response Rates**

Response rates are a source of concern on three counts. First, if the response rate to an enquiry is low the cost of the survey inevitably rises. The second concern is that the representativeness of the sample interviewed may be compromised and will need to be tested. Finally, in some markets where there are a limited number of eligible respondents – as in the case of some industrial markets – low response rates may make it difficult or impossible to complete the survey.

Participating in a market research survey is rarely a popular activity (though many respondents admit after the experience that they actually enjoyed it). Wherever respondents are approached their first concerns are whether they are qualified to provide the answers required and whether they can spare the amount of time the interview will take. There are very few opportunities to approach respondents when they are not in the midst of doing something else, be it shopping, housework, preparing or eating meals, watching television or any other activity which may be regarded as more important, or at least more urgent, than participating in a survey. The response to time constraints can either be to select an approach which minimises the amount of intrusion on respondents' time, such as a short telephone interview, or to maximise the opportunity to persuade respondents to cooperate, such as a skilled personal interviewer. Recourse may also be made to a technique which can generate a higher level of interest and enthusiasm, such as CATI and CAPI systems and the internet.

In industrial surveys, additional problems may be encountered. These include:

- voicemail
- company policy to research enquiries
- concerns about data protection.

Voicemail

Voicemail, particularly prevalent in the USA but increasingly used in Europe, is the sworn enemy of telephone research. For telephone research to work it must be possible to reach potential respondents relatively easily. Those who screen their calls using their voicemail systems will rarely return calls made by researchers, regardless of the content of the messages. It could be argued that voicemail is no different to the secretary defending access to her boss and while this is true for senior staff, voicemail extends the 'gate guardianship' function to all employees. The response to voicemail is to find new methods of approaching employees targeted for research and to make the reasons for cooperating more compelling.

Company policy

Company policy not to permit staff to cooperate in market research surveys is increasingly cited as a reason for refusing interviews. Whether true or not, it is certainly effective as there is no obvious antidote. A desire by employers to ensure that staff do not waste time on external enquiries and to reduce the risk that staff might give away commercially sensitive information is entirely understandable but a blanket ban on cooperation is surprising, especially in the case of companies that themselves commission market research. The response can be to solicit cooperation from management in a position to override policy by explaining the purpose of the survey and establishing the bonafides of the research organisation carrying out the project.

Data protection

Data protection and other legislation designed to protect consumers is a growing source of concern for market researchers. Most of the legislation is aimed at curbing the worst excesses of telesales organisations but can be interpreted as a restriction on research enquiries. In Europe and the USA legislation is being passed to:

- permit individuals to indicate that they do not wish to receive unsolicited telephone calls
- regulate the use of autodiallers
- regulate the acquisition and dissemination of personal information found in databases and voting lists
- limit the availability of telephone subscriber lists
- prevent researchers from monitoring telephone interviews by research company employees
- prevent selling under the guise of market research ('Sugging').

While some of the legislation is designed to help the research industry, and is supported by it, the unfortunate by-product is that many respondents do not distinguish between research and telemarketing and use legislation (or even rumours of legislation) as a reason for non-cooperation. Questionnaire and interviewer briefings need to include key statements that could put respondents' minds at rest. These can cover the difference between eliciting information and selling and the fact that all data collected by market research remains confidential to the research company and is not passed on to the research sponsor, except in aggregated form.

There is an impression that it is becoming harder to persuade respondents to cooperate in market research surveys. This is certainly true in some heavily researched industries but for most research the difficulties of obtaining responses from busy and cynical consumers and company employees have always been there. In fact the proportion of the population that has been asked to participate in a survey is surprisingly low and the universe is continuously changing as new consumers come into the market and employees change jobs. Nevertheless, survey resistance can have an adverse effect on research and is probably one of the main arguments for the use of non-invasive techniques (such as EPOS data and metering) wherever possible. If the use of large-scale, quantitative interview programmes is reduced there will be less chance of smaller-scale qualitative research being frustrated by non-cooperation.

13.8 Accuracy Levels Required

Accuracy effects the research mix by determining the scale of the interview programme. High levels of accuracy require large numbers of interviews and drive the project designer towards techniques which can be applied cost-effectively on a large scale. They may also require a more rigorous research procedure to ensure that all segments of a market are accurately reflected in the sample.

13.9 Geographical Scope

Wide geographical coverage, particularly international surveys, can have a similar effect on the research mix as accuracy in terms of increasing the scale of the survey and increasing the attraction of low-cost, large-scale techniques at the expense of in-depth approaches. International surveys may also require the use of multiple agencies, or fieldforces located in the countries being covered. This complicates the research process to the extent that it requires considerable coordination skills to ensure that the research is carried out consistently. To overcome the problems of coordination it is possible to carry out international telephone interview programmes from a single location resourced with multi-lingual interviewers. This approach has become increasingly attractive as international telephone charges have fallen, but there still comes a point where the number of interviews is so high that the additional costs in telephone bills cannot be justified by the benefits of a single research contractor. There are also some parts of the world where the telephone approach is itself unacceptable and where the charges are too high for a central location approach to be viable.

13.10 **Research Resources Available**

In the commercial research world it is reasonable to expect research agencies to have access to whatever resources are required to carry out surveys to the specifications decided. Surveys which are carried internally by companies or other research users are more likely to be in a position of having to adjust what they do to suit the resources at their disposition. The main limitation will be the availability of people with sufficient skills to design the survey, carry out fieldwork and analyse the results.

There was a time when internal research departments could be substantial organisations in their own right and better endowed with resources than many outside specialists. Those days came to an end in the earliest waves of downsizing, retrenching to core competencies and outsourcing, although some of the former internal organisations have survived as successful independent research agencies.

14 International Research

As markets develop globally there is a growing requirement for **global information**. Research can be carried out in most, if not all, countries and research services are available on a global scale either through multi-national research groups or independent local research companies. Whereas some years ago market research would have been an alien concept in certain cultures, increasing use has made it acceptable virtually everywhere.

National surveys which examine markets in a single country are rarely problematical. However, multi-national surveys, seeking comparable results in two or more countries do generate significant problems. Such surveys need to be planned with considerable care to ensure that recorded differences in attitude and approach reflect market conditions and not differences in survey approach. There is an increasing trend towards international surveys which are set up, analysed and reported centrally but with fieldwork carried out separately in each market. These have the major advantage of a common approach and harmonised analysis and are generally less costly than a series of individual country surveys.

Given the enormous differences between countries, research surveys are surprisingly similar in approach and structure world-wide. When defining international surveys the problems are more of adaptation to suit local conditions in each country than the adoption of completely different approaches and techniques. The factors which dictate differences in research are similar to those which influence international marketing – namely, language, literacy, culture and cultural traditions, religion, income levels, the stage of economic development, living conditions, distribution channels, legislation and regulation. Separately or collectively they can mean that what it is possible to do in one country is difficult or impossible to do in another. They also enhance the need for research to be carried out (Box 14.1) for unless the impact of such factors are fully understood local marketing plans will be inappropriate and ineffective.

14.1 Effect of Cultural Divergence on Research Objectives

Marketing issues and market conditions are sufficiently similar in European countries and the USA for a common survey design to be broadly workable. Differences in culture and business practice may suggest some changes in objectives but if the survey sponsor needs to make comparisons between

> **Box 14.1 Planning the international research programme**
>
> There are a number of issues which require careful consideration when planning an international research programme.
>
> - Effect of cultural divergence on research objectives
> - Matching the research techniques to local cultural conditions
> - Central location or distributed field research programmes
> - Availability and quality of research resources
> - International research logistics
> - Countries to be covered
> - Cost of international research.

countries, and therefore requires the use of a common questionnaire, these differences can be normally overlooked without seriously undermining the credibility of the research programme.

The problems really arise in research programmes aimed at the Middle Eastern, Far Eastern, Latin American and African countries where cultural and marketing conditions are so different – from each other as well as from Europe – that research objectives must be modified in order to be able to make sense of the findings. The effects of the global marketing activities of multi-nationals are tending to reduce the differences between countries and in many industrial markets the differences may already be minimal, but for the vast majority of consumer markets the research objectives need to take account of significant variations in need, taste, packaging, distribution channels, purchasing practices, readership habits and customer attitudes.

14.2 **Matching Research Techniques To Local Cultural Conditions**

Culture, which has been defined as the 'collective programming of the mind', has a fundamental effect on the acceptance of research approaches. Any categorisation of cultures identifies fundamental differences which will affect willingness to respond to questions, the methods by which questions can be asked and the accuracy of the responses that are likely to be obtained. Richard Lewis[1] distinguishes between linear-active, multi-active cultures and reactive cultures (Box 14.2).

The comprehension of market research and its objectives, a determinant of willingness to respond, is also affected by whether cultures are **data orientated** or **dialogue orientated**.

The **data orientated cultures**, such as the Americans, Swedes, Germans, Swiss and British, gather all relevant information before making decisions and are extensive users of the research process.

Box 14.2 Categorisation of culture

Linear-active cultures, typified by the Swedes, Swiss, Dutch and Germans, do one thing at a time on a scheduled timescale. They are disciplined and once persuaded to cooperate will make time to give full and accurate answers to questions. However, since they 'work by the book', obtaining cooperation may be frustrated by their interpretation of what is permissible for them to do and the information they are authorised to provide. There is an ever present fear that they may be censured for providing information.

Multi-active cultures are highly flexible and are less concerned with schedules, routines and punctuality. Typified by the Latin countries, they are less disciplined and carry on a number of tasks simultaneously and will become impatient with a long, highly structured enquiry. However, it is easier to break into their routines to question them and they will be less troubled by fears of stepping out of line that those in linear-active cultures. The main danger is that they will provide any answer that seems acceptable or show off their own creativity, regardless of its accuracy. Lewis developed a linear-active–multi-active scale:

Linear-Active

> Germans, Swiss
> Americans (WASP)
> Scandinavians, Austrians
> British, Canadians, New Zealanders
> Australians, South Africans
> Japanese
> Dutch, Belgians
> American subcultures (Jewish, Italian, Polish)
> French
> Czechs, Slovenians, Croats, Hungarians
> Northern Italians
> Chileans
> Russians, Other Slavs
> Portuguese
> Polynesians
> Spanish, Southern Italians, Mediterranean peoples
> Indians, Pakistanis
> Latin Americans, Arabs, Africans

Multi-Active

Reactive cultures

The members of reactive (or listening) cultures rarely initiate discussion and prefer to listen and think before deciding how to react. They rarely interrupt a speaker and will often ask clarification questions before responding. They prefer to avoid confrontation and are economical with words. Long silences and subtle body language replaces verbal communication to a significant extent and when words are used they tend to be semi-statements and roundabout statements rather than direct responses. Dialogue is difficult to establish. These cultures exist in Japan, Taiwan, Singapore, Korea, Turkey and Finland and are the source of the characterisation of these countries as 'inscrutable'. Reactive cultures are a nightmare for qualitative researchers and are hard work for quantitative research. Although accurate responses may be obtained in the end they will be monosyllabic rather than full and will exclude any volunteered elaborations.

Dialogue orientated cultures, such as the Latin countries, Arabs and Indians, are informed by their networks of contacts and base their own decisions on discussions and gossip rather than formal data collection exercises. They tend to see market research as an irrelevance and display more reluctance than others to participate in surveys.

The more specific issues which affect the use of research techniques are:

- availability and accuracy of secondary sources
- language and translation issues
- acceptability of research techniques
- attitudes to providing information.

Availability and accuracy of secondary sources

Published data from all types of sources are generally better in terms of coverage and accuracy in Europe and North America than in the rest of the world. While international sources may cover all countries in the same level of detail, the key national government sources may produce census and economic data to varying levels of accuracy and detail. There can also be enormous variations in the quality of other local sources, such as directories. The extent to which they vary is impossible to predict and there are always surprises. In Russia and the former Eastern European countries where information flows have been heavily influenced by politics, the current supply of statistics is surprisingly good.

The lack of accurate census data has a fundamental impact on survey design. If the structure of a consumer or industrial universe cannot be described, quota samples cannot be used. This throws the emphasis on random sampling. However, lists from which to draw samples may not be available or if they are, may be completely inaccurate. Industrial market research in Russia is severely hampered by the fact that the telephone numbers on almost all lists of companies are wrong.

Language and translation issues

Language – or, more specifically, the difficulty of translating questionnaires accurately – is a major issue for researchers. The difficulty arises from the need to capture precisely the same meaning in each country. This is difficult enough in normal documents but it requires extra special attention in the case of questionnaires where words need to be chosen carefully to ensure that respondents place the same interpretation on them. The problems of translation can be compounded by differences in literacy levels and may require solutions which rely more on pictorial images than words.

Acceptability of research techniques

Telephone interviews, personal interviews and self-completion questionnaires are not equally acceptable in all countries. Apart from variations in telephone ownership, which clearly affects the acceptability of telephone samples, in Far Eastern countries (where relationships tend to be more formal) the telephone is substantially less acceptable to respondents as a means of providing information. The use of the telephone for research is also a particular problem in Russia. Even in businesses, most of which do have a telephone, telephonists and secretaries show a marked reluctance to connect interviewers to management. The problems are not limited to developing or problem countries. In the USA the rapid growth in voicemail is, as we saw, acting as a severe hindrance to telephone surveys. It is no longer possible to get through to a high proportion of respondents at the first attempt.

Differences in attitudes towards street interviews and permitting strangers into the home can clearly affect the application of personal interview programmes. In many countries security problems have given rise to a growth in estates or compounds to which entry is restricted. The level of protection has increased for middle- and upper-class residences in South Africa, South East Asian countries and even the USA as crime rates and levels of social unrest have increased.

Response rates to self-completion questionnaires are influenced by literacy rates, the quality of the postal service and variations in attitude towards the completion of forms. A questionnaire which might work well in a disciplined market such as Germany with a high-quality postal service can prove to be a waste of time in other European countries, such as Italy.

Attitudes to providing information

In contrast to the openness of the American consumer, as outlined above, in some cultures secrecy and confidentiality are still regarded as important and results in a reluctance to discuss any topics with strangers. Even in Europe, the publicity given to data protection and a series of invasion of privacy issues has created a climate in which respondents are more reluctant to cooperate in surveys. Business intelligence enquiries in Germany will commonly be stonewalled on the grounds that they infringe German data protection legislation. Elsewhere the sex of the interviewer or their social origins may influence willingness to participate in a survey. In Muslim countries it is virtually impossible for a man to interview a woman and in India there would be serious problems if an interviewer from one caste tried to interview a respondent from another.

Problems of data collection can frequently arise when the questioning relates to financial matters. Ignorance due to a failure to keep adequate financial records and, more commonly, suspicion that the enquiry has some official motivation can make respondents inordinately reluctant to discuss such matters with interviewers regardless of the assurances given.

14.3 Central Location or Distributed Field Research Programmes

Consideration of the above issues would tend to suggest that survey organisation and field research is best carried out 'in-country'. This approach ensures that full account is taken of local conditions and although it imposes timing, cost and logistical penalties; there would have to be a very strong case for attempting a multi-national consumer survey from a central location. For industrial surveys the situation is different. The conditions within industrial markets are sufficiently similar for interviewers conversant in the local languages to be able to cope. Companies and institutions active in major markets such as telecommunications, information technology, construction, healthcare provision and engineering operate on similar principles world-wide and assessing their needs, practices and attitudes poses few insurmountable research problems. In these cases, the advantages of centrally organised research programmes can be taken advantage of.

The centralisation of the research process generally means that the research can be carried out more quickly and at lower cost than a distributed research programme. There are fewer opportunities for differences in interpretation between the national contractors, there is no need for multiple briefings and there are opportunities to carry over the lessons learned in one country to others as the research programme progresses.

14.4 Availability and Quality of Research Resources

The research business has developed globally and there are very few countries that do not have an indigenous research business. In many cases national research companies are subsidiaries or licensees of European or US research organisations and should therefore offer the same standards of research and diversity of research techniques that are to be found in their home markets. However, not all services may prove to be available – for example, in many countries the demand for continuous research programmes is insufficient to justify their establishment and panel data is therefore unavailable.

Identifying and selecting suitable research agencies for international projects is similar to that adopted at home, made difficult only by remoteness and lack of familiarity. The simple tests outlined in Chapter 18 apply just as well in foreign markets as they do at home. Clients often side-step the problem by selecting a domestic research contractor and relying on them to identify suitable foreign sub-contractors. In this sense the international research companies have a clear advantage since they claim familiarity with their sister companies and demonstrate that similar practices and quality controls are implemented. The only danger is that the local subsidiaries of international groups are not all equally appropriate for the research being considered. The services they offer and their client experience will be conditioned by local management and the types of research they have chosen to concentrate on. This can result in companies being force-fitted into a multinational research programme for which they are unsuited. Independent research contractors have greater freedom to select the most suitable partners for the research though they too will tend to use their friends rather than companies with which they are unfamiliar but may have more appropriate experience. If commissioning an international survey through a domestic research company it is essential to know who they are proposing to use as their sub-contractors, their background and related experience.

14.5 International Research Logistics

The increased complexity of international surveys means that the research process must be subject to more rigorous controls if the outcome is to be satisfactory. In this sense centrally organised surveys have a distinct advantage since they are carried out by the same team of research executives. Surveys in which the research is sub-contracted to local partners provide far more scope for error and delay. In order to assure success there must be a strong management team controlling the survey and a clear understanding of who is responsible for what (Box 14.3).

The briefing and review processes are of critical importance, since they ensure that the results are consistent and that any divergences in results between countries reflect local market conditions and not differences in the way the methodology has been applied.

14.6 Countries to be Covered

Obviously the number and location of countries to be covered by a research programme will have a major effect on its complexity and cost. There have to be strong marketing reasons for commissioning a survey which covers a large number of countries simultaneously and in equal depth. Unless all of the data is to be used soon after the survey is completed and whilst it is still current, the cost of such a programme may be hard to justify (Box 14.4).

Box 14.3 Contractors and sub-contractors

The process which appears to work best involves:

- **Main contractor**, responsible for:
  - definition of survey objectives
  - design of questionnaires
  - preliminary translation of questionnaires
  - sample design and sampling procedures
  - pilot questionnaires
  - briefing of local sub-contractors
  - data entry and analysis
  - review of findings with sub-contractors
  - reporting of findings
  - client liaison.

- **Sub-contractors**, responsible for:
  - local secondary research
  - checking questionnaire translations
  - local pilot survey
  - suggesting modifications to questionnaire and research approach
  - local interviewing
  - submitting questionnaires or data files to main contractors.

Box 14.4 The international research budget

Common approaches to conserving the international research budget are:

- Commissioning an overview of a large number of countries in order to identify those which appear to be worth studying in depth and **ranking them in order of attractiveness**; such overviews may rely on secondary sources and limited numbers of interviews with local 'expert' respondents rather than a sample survey
- Selecting countries which appear to be representative of the different types of market conditions which exist and **extrapolating the results** to remaining markets; when looking at Europe many multinationals research the top four countries (France, Germany, Italy and the UK) and then select sample small countries such as the Netherlands, Switzerland or Sweden.

14.7 Costs of International Research

The cost of carrying out market research varies considerably from country to country and depending on the nationality of the company commissioning the research will tend to appear either good value or extremely expensive. Japan is the country in which research costs are highest, with budgets 2–3 times those required in Europe for the same size and scope of project. Research costs in Europe can also vary by a factor of two between countries and tend to be lowest in the UK. US research costs are generally on a par with those in the UK. Elsewhere, research costs are influenced by the degree of local competition, the difficulty of carrying out research and the level of interest in carrying out research for foreign clients.

14.8 Support for International Research

Many governments, eager to promote exports, offer subsidies for organisations carrying out international market research. In the UK the Export Market Research Scheme provides a subsidy of between 30 per cent and 60 per cent of the cost of surveys to explore export markets. Difference in the level of subsidy depends on whether it is a private company, a consortium of companies or a trade association (who get the highest subsidy) which commissions the survey.

Note

1   Richard Lewis, *When Cultures Collide* (London: Nicholas Brealey Publishing, 1996).

15 Analysis of Findings

The final stage in the research process is the analysis of findings. In large-scale quantitative surveys this is normally undertaken mechanically using survey analysis packages. Qualitative surveys, where the samples are smaller and the responses are unstructured, are generally analysed by hand. Small sample quantitative surveys and those carried out for business intelligence programmes may also be hand analysed or entered into a spreadsheet to avoid the set-up time and cost required for computer analysis. The output, be it tables or qualitative description, is reported to the research user in a report which interprets the findings and draws conclusions. The report is the prime record of what has been done and represents the **final tangible outcome** from the research.

The key steps by which questionnaires are converted from raw data to finished tabulations of results are described in this chapter together, with some of the analysis techniques that can be used. Statistics play a large role in research analysis and there are many forms of statistical analysis that can be used. Some are relatively simple and others exceedingly complex. A very high proportion of research analysis makes use of the simplest and most straightforward statistical techniques. Reports which move much beyond the calculation of averages and percentages and tests for statistical significance are the exception rather than the rule. However, there is a growing role for more complex analysis such as simple and multiple regression, conjoint and correspondence analysis, and they are therefore also described. The text concentrates on what the analyses are designed to do rather than to explaining how to compute them. For those wishing to carry out statistical analysis for themselves, any good statistical textbook will provide the necessary formulae or the reader can acquire a statistical analysis package.

15.1 Controls

Before analysing any questionnaires they must be subjected to a series of careful controls to ensure that they are complete and accurate. Any rogue questionnaires will distort the findings or tabulations and can result in researchers spending considerable amounts of time trying to reconcile the data. The control procedures that may be required are set out below. The physical control of questionnaires is not normally required if CATI, CAPI and CASI systems have been used, but are essential in the case of all manually applied questionnaires.

Editing

Editing is a mechanical process which is carried out to check that all questions have been answered, that the skip patterns have been followed correctly, that all open-ended questions have been filled in and that the data that has been entered is legible. Interviewers often complete questionnaires in situations and at locations where recording the responses is difficult. Although interviewers are required to transcribe the results to ensure that they can be read, their efforts may not be wholly successful. Any interviews which prove incomplete or appear to contain inaccurate or inconsistent data need to be returned to the field department for checking and completion.

Verification

The verification process is concerned with the accuracy of the data that has been collected from each respondent. It includes checks to ensure that the interviews have been carried out properly and that the answers are correct and consistent within the questionnaire. In telephone surveys verification includes a programme of call backs to a small sample of respondents to ensure that they were indeed interviewed, that they fitted the sampling criteria and that the recorded responses are correct. Call backs can be carried out for personal street and in-home interviews but only if the identity and telephone number of respondents has been collected.

Verification is also required to check for impossible or improbable answers and that the arithmetic in questions involving additions or percentages is accurate. Open-ended questions require careful scrutiny to ensure that respondents have answered the questions in the way that was intended. Questions which seem perfectly clear at the questionnaire drafting stage can prove to have several different interpretations when the questionnaire is applied. For example, an open-ended question which asks why respondents shop at a particular grocery store will normally elicit replies such as 'it is close', 'it has the best range of products' or the prices are competitive'. However, some respondents may reply 'to buy groceries' – perfectly accurate but not the type of response that was required.

Coding

The coding process assigns codes to the various categories of response that could not be pre-coded. The need arises in the case of unstructured and semi-structured questionnaires which contain open-ended questions. It involves an initial analysis of a sample of responses in order to determine the categories of reply that have been given and to assign codes to those that appear most frequently. The process requires some skill if carried out by hand but can be simplified by the use of software which recognises key words and automatically assigns codes to statements which include them (see below).

15.2 Data Entry

Once controlled, responses to questions need to be entered into a format which permits analysis. Typically when paper questionnaires have been used this will involve a keyboard transfer to a floppy or hard disk using a data entry software package such as SPSS Data Entry of the front end of an analysis package such as SNAP. The data entry can also design a form which acts both as the questionnaire and an online entry form. The use of CATI, CAPI or CASI systems make a separate data entry process redundant.

For highly structured questionnaires **optical scanning** provides a quick and reliable alternative to keyboard entry. Scanning can cope with open ended responses, by copying the written responses into a file for subsequent analysis, but it is most effective when applied to questionnaires on which the responses consist of check marks in boxes. To use scanning, the questionnaire has to be designed in advance for the optical scanning programme that is to be used, the principal concern being that there are suitable locator marks to ensure that all boxes are positioned at the points the software expects to find them.

Hand tabulation, or content analysis, is used when the responses are entirely open ended and the number of questionnaires is small. Where large numbers of open-ended responses have been collected they can be computer analysed using programmes like SPSS's TextSmart. This classifies open-ended responses into categories by recognising key works. By taking the chore out of the analysis process these packages make open-ended questions that are analysed into simple classifications a practical possibility on large-scale surveys.

15.3 Analysis

A wide range of survey analysis packages are available to run on all types of computer hardware. They vary considerably in cost and sophistication but all of them will produce basic market research tabulations. The most common functions are:

- counts
- statistical analysis
- cross-tabulations
- tests for statistical significance
- measures of association
- charting
- entry of verbatim comments which can be printed out by category of respondent.

Bases and counts

The basic form of analysis for quantitative research is a count of the total number of respondents that have replied to each question (the base) and the breakdown of the total between the various options contained in the question. In a simple question offering 'yes' and 'no' as alternatives, the analysis will present the numbers responding 'yes' and the number responding 'no'. The same applies where respondents are offered more complex options, such as the shops from which they have made purchases, the prices they paid or the makes and models of equipment they purchased. Care must be taken to distinguish between questions to which only one response is permitted – namely, the only option which applies – and those to which multiple responses are possible. For example, questions on readership may require respondents to identify all the journals they read or the three journals they read most frequently.

In setting up the analysis provision must be made to record the 'don't knows' or 'unanswered'. Not all respondents will be able to answer all questions, either because they have forgotten or the question is seeking information which is outside their experience. There may also be a level of unwillingness to answer questions. The proportion of unanswered questions is an important control on the quality of the data. In an extreme case a high proportion of 'don't knows' can invalidate any conclusions which are drawn from the responses.

Statistical analysis

The numerical counts are normally used to compute **percentages** (the percentage responding 'yes' and 'no') together with a series of descriptive statistics. The most common descriptors are the arithmetic **means** (averages), **modes** (the most commonly occurring values), **medians** (the middle value, or the value below which 50 per cent of the observations lie), the **range** (the difference between the highest and the lowest value) and the **frequency distribution** (the spread of responses over the values measured). These are simple calculations which all need to be considered in order to determine the 'quality' of the data that has been obtained and the reliance that can be placed on it. For example, in a customer satisfaction survey requiring respondents to rate the performance of a supplier on a scale of 1 to 5, where 5 equals excellent performance and 1 equals poor performance there is a significant difference between the two sets of data in Box 15.1 covering samples of 30 companies, even though the averages are the same.

The customers of supplier 1 are far more consistent in their ratings, the majority giving scores of 3 or 4. Supplier 2 has more highly satisfied customers but also a lot more dissatisfied customers and therefore more to worry about than supplier 1. The extent to which the results diverge can be

Box 15.1 Divergence of results

Number scoring	Supplier 1	Supplier 2
1	1	2
2	1	5
3	11	5
4	16	11
5	1	7
Average score	3.5	3.5
Mode	4	4
Median	4	4
Standard deviation	0.777	1.224

computed using the formula for **standard deviation**. The lower the standard deviation the higher the level of clustering of the responses around a single value.

Cross-tabulations

The analysis of the total sample contacted is interesting in itself but the full value of a survey is gained only when the results are computed for **each category of respondent** that has been interviewed. Cross-tabulations show the responses to questions according to breakdowns revealed in other questions. The most common-cross tabulations show the breakdown or responses according to the demographic data collected at the beginning of questionnaires (such as age, sex, income group, geodemographic sector, geographical location, industry sector or size of company). This analysis shows the variations in response that have arisen in the segments of the market that have been covered.

Cross-tabulations can also be constructed retrospectively using any combinations of questions to provide further detail in the patterns observed. For example the analysis of a questionnaire which asks the brands of product purchased and the readership of magazines can include a cross-tabulation which shows magazine readership by those purchasing each brand.

The danger with cross-tabulations is that although the total sample may be adequate for the purpose of the survey, the numbers of responses being analysed for any set of cross-tabulations may be too small to produce results which are statistically significant.

Tests for statistical significance

In any set of statistical tabulations the fact that the numbers differ does not mean that the differences between them (large or small) are **statistically significant**. Statistical significance occurs when the difference between the values is unlikely to have arisen by chance and must therefore be accepted as a **real difference**. In the case of research results, it is essential to show that the difference between two figures cannot have arisen purely as a result of sampling error. Significance can be stated in degrees of certainty depending on the probability of it existing. There are a number of tests for statistical significance which can be used. The most common tests used in research are the Chi-Square Test, the Kolmogorov–Smirnov test and the 'sign test'.

Measures of association

Measures of association show whether a relationship exists between two or more independently derived sets of data. In market research it is commonly necessary to show whether marketing strategies are effective. This can be deduced if it can be shown that there is a relationship between **independent variables** (such as price and promotional expenditure) and **dependent variables** (such as sales growth). The fact that a relationship exists does not prove that sales growth has occurred because of a price reduction or an increase in promotional expenditure, but it does *suggest* that the strategy is having the desired effect.

The most common measures of association are:

- **Simple regression** – which measures the correlation between two variables
- **Multivariate analysis** – which examines the relationships between many variables.

Simple regression

Simple regression analysis shows whether there is a positive or negative linear or curvilinear relationship between the two variables. The **correlation coefficient** shows the strength of the relationship that exists.

The results can be particularly useful when making projections of demand. If, as is likely, it can be demonstrated that there are measurable correlations between consumers' expenditure and the purchases of washing powder, independently derived forecasts of consumers' expenditure can be used to make projections of washing powder sales. The process is not quite as simple as it sounds, but is a reasonable starting point. Other factors have to be fed into the equation since the degree of correlation is likely to change over time (such as the effect of improved technology in washing machines on reducing the volume of washing powder) and with increases or decreases in income levels (causing a greater or lesser use of commercial laundry services).

Multivariate analysis

Multivariate analysis comprises a series of techniques, of which the most commonly used are:

- multiple regression analysis
- factor analysis
- cluster analysis
- perceptual maps
- conjoint analysis.

Multiple regression analysis calculates the relationship between one dependent variable and a series of independent variables. The analysis shows the extent to which the independent variables explain the variations in the dependent variable. Continuing the example quoted above in which simple regression analysis showed the relationship between consumers' expenditure and sales of washing powder, multiple regression analysis can be used to show the extent to which washing powder sales are influenced by a number of other independent variables, such as population growth, the number of children, average income levels, sales of washing machines and the promotional expenditure of washing powder manufacturers. In other words, it can be used to construct a **model which explains the effect** of all the dynamic forces which have an impact on the sales of washing powder.

Factor analysis is used to group large numbers of variables into a smaller number of associated variables (factors) which collectively explain how respondents feel about a product, organisation or event. For example, in customer satisfaction surveys, data is collected to show how supplier performance is perceived on a wide range of product and service attributes. The analysis can cover 20–30 attributes with average performance scores being computed for each attribute. Factor analysis is used to identify the groups of attributes which collectively describe how the respondents feel about the supplier. The 20–30 attributes can typically be grouped into three or four factors, each of which can be given a description depending on the attributes which are contained within it. These might be product factors, if there is a strong association between various product characteristics, personnel factors if they are people-related, service factors if they are service related, and so on. The analysis also shows the extent to which each factor contributes towards the overall perception of the supplier in percentage terms (such as factor 1 = 68 per cent, factor 2 = 20 per cent and factor 3 = 10 per cent).

Cluster analysis is used to separate respondents into homogeneous groups that have common characteristics. Its primary use is in market segmentation analysis where it is essential to spot groups which have similar product or service requirements and can be approached in similar ways. The clusters are commonly named and their attributes described.

Perceptual mapping, as the name implies, provides a picture or a map of a marketplace which defines the perceptions respondents have of products, brands, services or companies. The technique defines the key characteristics by which products, brands, etc. could be described and locates the products or brands on these dimensions in accordance with the respondents' perceptions.

The technique shows the **perceived differences** between products or brands. Minimal differences, which show up as products or brands mapped in close proximity, indicate strong competition; large differences, which show up as products or brands in isolation on the map, indicate uniqueness in the marketplace. The results need to be combined with market structure data in order to show whether the territory which the products or brands are perceived as occupying is that in which the supplier wishes to be. Perceptual maps can be created from scales on which respondents evaluate the specific attributes of products or brands. These can be numerical rating scales. In order to convert the rating information to a perceptual map, it is necessary to use multidiscriminate analysis, multidimensional scaling or factor analysis programmes.

Perceptual maps are most useful for:

- concept development
- product positioning decisions
- segmentation analysis
- strengths and weakness analysis.

Conjoint analysis produces estimates of the 'utilities', or values, which respondents attach to specific product features or service attributes. The best combination of features or attributes (the consumers' ideal product) is that which results in the highest total of utilities – or, put another way, the highest level of customer satisfaction. The relationship between the best and any other combination is clearly shown by the reduction in total utility that results. Conjoint analysis is used extensively in product design and increasingly to determine the service packages which will maximise suppliers' performance.

Conjoint analysis is far better than rating scales at identifying the real requirements of customers. On rating scales respondents can give high values to all of the attributes they are presented with, which generally results in an overweighting of those which are in fact of low importance. In real life consumers have to make choices between alternative features. Conjoint analysis simulates this process by presenting respondents with a series of paired product or service variables between which they have to choose. Its main research advantage is that it provides an **independent weighting of each attribute** – i.e. one which is not influenced by the other attributes that are being covered.

Conjoint analysis can be carried out in a number of different ways but the most common involve the pairing of individual attributes (preference-based or adaptive conjoint) or the pairing of complete product descriptions (choice-based or full profile conjoint). Some researchers regard the choice-based approach as being more realistic, since in real life purchasers choose between complete products not individual product attributes. They also feel that it is a better process for handling price, since prices relate only to complete products. Whilst these points are clearly valid there are many situations in which the choice-based approach is too restricting, particularly in terms of the number of product and service features that can be included in the various product descriptions. The number of attributes can be increased in the choice-based approach if the conjoint is administered by computer but if this is not feasible and the number of features to be considered is high, preference-based conjoint is the better alternative.

In order to weight individual attributes the supplier must first define of all those that he wishes to consider. A luxury automobile, for example, can be defined as in Box 15.2.

The number of attributes that can be covered is limited by the number of pairings they create and the abilities of the analysis software. A matrix of the above size requires respondents to choose between 700 pairings whereas a matrix of 50 attributes creates a requirement for approximately 2300 pairings. These numbers can be handled by some of the specialist software that has been developed[1] (primarily by reducing the workload placed on each respondent) but is beyond the capacity of others.

Box 15.2 Attribute definition

Attribute	Level 1	Level 2	Level 3	Level 4
Horse power (bhp)	350	300	250	200
Fuel	Petrol	Diesel	–	–
Fuel consumption (mpg)	30	25	20	15
Maximum speed (mph)	150	140	130	120
Acceleration (0 to 60 mph) (sec)	5	6	7	8
Transmission	Automatic	Manual	–	–
Seats	Leather	Fabric	–	–
Climate control	Full aircon	Heating only	–	–
Service interval (miles)	9000	10,000	11,000	–

The choice-based approach simplifies the analysis problems by presenting respondents with fewer options of complete automobile specifications such as:

- Option 1   350 bhp, petrol, automatic, 150 mph, full airconditioning
- Option 2   300 bhp, petrol, manual, 140 mph, heating only
- Option 3   250 bhp, diesel, automatic, 130 mph, heating only
- Option 4   200 hp, diesel, manual, 120 mph, full airconditioning

The simulation will show the proportion of respondents preferring each model option and, by using a computer-based interview technique, can also determine the effect on model attractiveness of changing one or more of the variables. This is particularly useful if prices are added to the specification.

In either approach, the key to the success of the technique lies in the **selection of the attributes** that are to be covered. It is common to select a hierarchy of attributes ranging from the best to the worst so that the degradation in customer utility can be measured. A hierarchy is not essential, it can also be valuable to measure alternative characteristics to test their value. For example, in a conjoint programme aimed at testing the acceptability of alternative service packages, delivery and billing procedures might feature. For delivery there is usually a clear hierarchy of options such as same day, following day, two days and one week. Conjoint analysis will show the premium, if any, that respondents attach to rapid delivery and the extent to which satisfaction reduces as delivery dates are stretched. Billing can normally be monthly or quarterly and based on summary bills or detailed itemised bills. With these attributes there is no obvious degradation in service, only a difference in approach.

Clearly any attributes that are not included in the conjoint analysis will not be measured unless they lie between attributes that have been chosen – in which case their utilities can be interpolated. Care must be taken to exclude unrealistic attributes, such as heavy price discounts, since they will invariably attract scores which swamp the others. Whilst this is not a crippling disadvantage, since they can be ignored, they can distort the other utilities and it is preferable to confine the approach to attributes it is feasible to offer.

The selection of the attributes for inclusion in the conjoint analysis can be made either on the basis of technical research (which defines feasible options), an analysis of competing products available on the market, management experience or qualitative research amongst potential buyers.

Conjoint analysis can be used to define either the optimum product or service package for the market as a whole, or the product or service characteristics which will have greatest appeal in each segment of a market. This is achieved by segmenting the sample and running a separate conjoint analysis **within each segment** or by using the conjoint results as a basis for cluster analysis which shows the relationship between attributes and customer types.

One of the most valuable aspects of conjoint analysis is that it provides a basis for modelling which is durable and can be reused for as long as the fundamental characteristics of customer requirements remain relatively undisturbed (for example, by the introduction of radically new technology). The attractiveness of conjoint analysis has increased as it has become easier to administer. The availability of proprietary techniques (such as Simalto and SMART), but more importantly the introduction of standard conjoint analysis packages (such as those which can be purchased from Sawtooth Software), which have made conjoint analysis accessible to all competent researchers.

Charting

Charting can make an important contribution to the speed at which research results can be assimilated. Pictures do speak louder than words, primarily by conveying the **spatial relationship** between the sets of data that have been collected. The high and low points in a data set will stand out far more clearly on a bar chart than in a table and a line chart provides a more effective presentation of trends than a series of growth rates. Correlations can be seen more clearly in scatter diagrams.

Most analysis packages will create charts from the tabulations they produce and over time the complexity of these charts has tended to increase by taking into account more variables and plotting on multiple scales. It is worth remembering that whilst most research users will benefit from simple charts they may be left completely baffled by three- and four-dimensional images with complex scales even when they are carefully explained. If this happens, the value of producing the charts is undermined.

Verbatim comments

Verbatim comments are an important part of any analysis. Although open-ended responses may be used to create tables the inclusion of verbatim comments in the text of the report adds authenticity and colour to the findings.

15.4 **Market Forecasting**

Forecasting is a highly developed science which meets the need for market planners to see **what is coming** rather than what has already occurred. The market research techniques described above can measure only what exists or what has happened in the past. To determine what is likely to happen in the future requires a separate set of techniques.

Sales or market forecasts can use a variety of inputs, of which the most important are:

- trend analysis
- economic and environmental forecasts
- correlations
- market modelling
- surveys of customer purchasing intentions
- expert opinion
- technological forecasting.

Trend analysis

Where time series exist trend analysis is the simplest method of forecasting, provided it can be shown that what has happened in the past is likely to continue into the future. This method of forecasting is like driving a car by looking only into the rear view mirror: it works well until there is a bend in the road. Time series may provide some indication of forthcoming bends, but cannot take account of factors whose incidence and magnitude have not been previously and regularly experienced. Cyclical factors, such as the seasonal patterns of demand, will show up in the trend data but the effects of a major recession or abnormal weather patterns will not.

Economic and environmental forecasts

The process of market forecasting is assisted by the fact that in all countries a wide range of forecasts are produced for purposes which range from national financial planning to the allocation of local resources. These include economic forecasts covering gross national product (GNP), income levels, industrial output, construction activity, the balance of payments and unemployment. GNP forecasts include consumers' expenditure, which is directly relevant to projections of the sales of consumer products and services. Economic forecasts are prepared at regular intervals by ministries of finance, international organisations such as the OECD, by banks and by a wide variety of economic institutes. Secondary research will normally locate those which are relevant and available.

In addition to the economy professional forecasters also project trends in population, social trends, political stability and technological development. These, too, may be highly relevant to the future development of a market.

Correlations

The main application for economic and environmental forecasts is to act as independent variables from which market forecasts can be derived by correlation analysis. If a relationship can be shown to exist between the demand for products or product families and an economic variable such as consumers' expenditure, the economic forecast can be used as a basis for projecting product demand. The forecast will need to take account of the strength of the relationship and whether it is direct, leading or lagging in terms of timing.

Market modelling

Simple correlations may not provide sufficient explanations of market development, in which case it may be necessary to construct a model of the market into which a number of variables are integrated. Models can take account of the main drivers of demand such as population growth and income levels, the effects of shortages or surpluses of supply on prices and the impact of directly or indirectly competitive products.

Surveys of customer purchasing intentions

Asking customers to forecast their requirements produces data of only limited value, even if the forecast period is short. Purchasers do not routinely think about their future requirements and will generally assume that the future will be a continuation of the past. Nevertheless, surveys of purchasing intentions and consumer confidence can provide an indication of the direction and strength of demand trends. The correlation of past purchasing intention survey results with actual demand trends may make it possible to refine the technique by developing a set of weights which can be used to adjust future survey findings.

Expert opinion

Although individual customers may not analyse their future requirements, there are others active in marketplaces who do. Distributors, dealers, competitive suppliers and trade associations are in a position to observe trends and to form opinions on the directions in which demand is moving. Surveys of expert opinion carried out among such groups can provide a highly qualified view of the future of a market.

Technological forecasting

Although this book is concerned primarily with market analysis there is a closely associated requirement for forecasts of technologies – what is likely to emerge, which will be the 'winning' technologies, at what pace are the winners likely to be introduced and which companies are best positioned to make the breakthrough. Technological forecasting was developed by a number of 'think tanks', such as SRI and Battelle, to address these questions. The process involves the collection, synthesis, rationalisation and recycling of opinions of experts in the technologies under consideration, as well as those active in related areas. The base data are collected either by interviewing experts individually or by bringing them together into groups to discuss trends and likely developments. Obviously the quality of a forecast depends on the quality of the expertise that is fed into it. A major part of the forecasting process therefore consists of the identification of the experts that are to be consulted. While there is a need for individuals working at the leading edge of the relevant technologies there is also a requirement for experts who can project their thinking beyond current boundaries and draw scenarios of what might happen.

A technological forecast rarely provides a single answer. It normally describes a series of alternatives and weights the probability of each of them occurring. The forecast can prove to be self-fulfilling in the sense that if it identifies areas in which breakthroughs are both required and expected, the results may be used to focus the future activities of researchers, thereby causing the forecast developments!

Note

1   Probit Ltd, based in Newhaven, offers a conjoint analysis service which can handle up to 50 attributes.

16 Reporting Findings

No survey is complete until the results have been delivered to the client. Reporting is an integral part of the research process the importance of which can be easily overlooked by those whose primary enthusiasm is for data collection and analysis. Unfortunately, there are countless examples of good research being undermined by poor reporting and there are also examples of poor research being covered up by artistic reporting. Both are equally unacceptable to the research user.

The process of compiling a report can highlight data collection or analysis problems whilst there is still time to take corrective action. It can also identify weaknesses in the original objectives, such as a failure to specify items of information which are relevant to the problem, and thereby initiate actions to fill the gaps and forestall later questioning.

Report preparation and presentations are key skills which do not come naturally to all researchers, particularly those whose skills are more numerate and statistical and may be happier in the back rooms of research companies rather than explaining results to research users. This is no different to a production environment which includes staff who are excellent at making things but could not sell them to save their lives. Division of labour can be just as important in the research business as in manufacturing industry.

The delivery of results is normally made in the form of a written report supported by an oral presentation but it is increasingly common for research results to be provided in electronic format, either on disk or by e-mail, so that research users can integrate them into their internal information systems. Electronic delivery is also a useful method of delivering results quickly. Clients for television audience measurement require the previous night's viewing figures on their desks each morning and delivering them online represents a significant advance over the manual delivery of printed reports.

16.1 Reporting Objectives

However the results are delivered, the reporting process needs to achieve a minimum number of objectives. It should be **comprehensive** in terms of its coverage of the topics that were being addressed by the research, it should be **accurate** and it should **easy to assimilate** by management that does not always have time to pore over detailed tabulations. It is also worth remembering that in most surveys the written or electronic report is the only

171

durable evidence that the survey has been carried out. It will sit on library or office shelves long after the discussion of the results has been completed and any researcher who wishes to ensure that his or her services are reused should seek to ensure that the report acts as a durable testimonial.

Comprehensiveness

Comprehensiveness is the easiest to establish. A comparison between the original objectives of the research and the findings will show whether there are any gaps. It may be that not all of the objectives could be achieved, either because the research approach did not permit complete coverage (a problem more likely to arise in business intelligence approaches than in survey research) or because some of the data originally specified proved not to be relevant. In these cases, gaps in the data need to be explained so that the reader is not left wondering whether the data was omitted in error.

Accuracy

Accuracy is more difficult to demonstrate and to verify. There is always a risk of errors creeping into long and complex research exercises and research users rely on the fact that research suppliers will have checked their processes thoroughly in order to minimise, if not eliminate errors.

   The types of error that can arise are **data entry errors**, in which the data is inaccurately transferred from questionnaire to data file; **process errors**, resulting from the use of the wrong methods of calculation, **transcription errors**, which take place during the transfer of data from the analysis to the reports, and **errors of interpretation**. Higher levels of mechanisation in the collection, analysis and presentation of data should reduce the incidence of error but it would be foolhardy for any researcher to claim that error can be eliminated completely. Most of those responsible for checking reports, either in the research organisation or among the users of the results, rely on signals, sanity checks and consistency checks to indicate whether the results of the survey are correct. The most important signals lie within the reports themselves. Do the tables add up? Do all percentages add up to 100 (allowing for rounding errors)? Is the content of the tables consistent? Does the report contain an unacceptably high number of spelling errors? Sloppiness at this level may be indicative of more fundamental and unseen problems elsewhere.

Ease of assimilation

Ease of assimilation is a function of the format of the report, but also depends on the what the reader is used to. There are no hard and fast rules in this sense except that the use of clear, concise language will always be preferable to long complex constructions using excessive jargon and technical language. The report should also be formatted to take account of the requirements of the various audiences of readers (see **Length**, below).

16.2 Report Format

Reports tend to conform to certain conventions which have evolved over time to ensure that they are of maximum utility to their readers. This is not to say that all reports need to follow the same style. There are many ways of presenting data, any number of which could be equally acceptable in any given situation, but the style that is followed needs to be one which report writers/presenters and research users are equally comfortable with.

Some of the issues of report format which need to be considered are:

- length
- bullet points
- tabular material
- charts and diagrams
- appendices
- use of colour.

Length

Many researchers and research users **confuse report length with quality**. A weighty tome may also be regarded as representing value for money. In practice, a single sentence may convey all that is needed about the outcome of the research exercise. It would be a brave researcher that would act on this observation, but there is absolutely no case for producing a report which is longer than it needs to be to convey its message and convince the reader that the research has been conducted properly.

The length of report which is acceptable is commonly a function of the seniority of the reader. Senior management will read and use a report differently from junior staff and will become impatient if the report does not enable them to get to the essence of the findings quickly or provide them with an interpretation of what it all means. Junior staff tend to look for detail and for masses of data which they can use in their own analyses. These requirements can be easily reconciled by producing a short summary report and interpretation for senior management and a lengthy, detailed report for their subordinates.

Bullet points

Management schools and management consultants have introduced a synoptic style of report writing which relies on short, bullet point statements. There is no doubt that 'brevity is the soul of wit' but it is not always appropriate and care must be taken to ensure that the reader accepts the bullet point approach and will not feel short changed if a full explanatory text is not available. Bullet point reports have the advantage of being short and quick to read but to be effective they require a high order of writing skill. The bullet point approach can all too easily present the reader with a series of portentous and meaningless statements which fail to explain the market situation fully.

Tabular material

Market research analysis commonly produces reams of tables which present a complete analysis by category of respondent. In some situations it is the convention to compile the report largely from tables with a minimum of explanatory text, leaving readers to draw their own conclusions. The acceptability of this approach will depend on the numeracy and seniority of the readers. Tables can be completely baffling to some readers, particularly those not conversant with statistical terminology. More senior readers normally expect researchers to carry out the interpretative work for them and tell them what the tables are saying.

Charts and diagrams

Illustrations can be highly effective in reinforcing points, summarising patterns and transmitting data quickly particularly for those who can absorb spatial patterns more easily than strings of numerical data. Charts and diagrams also have the virtue of breaking up dense text and, by creating variety, make a report easier to assimilate.

As with words, the most valuable charts are those which are simple both to construct and to read. The most common forms of chart used in reports are:

- Pie charts
- Bar charts
- Line charts
- Radar charts
- Histograms
- Scatter diagrams
- Area charts
- Flow diagrams.

All of the above are standard features in spreadsheet and charting packages and are simple to create. Unfortunately the chart-makers can get carried away into the realms of multidimensional charts and complex structures which can take more time and effort to decipher than the raw data. There is little point in presenting charts which serve only to prove that the researcher has a labyrinthine and complex mind but do nothing to enhance the readers understanding of the data.

Appendices

Appendices containing technical information and data print-outs are a useful method of separating the conclusions from the supporting information. If they are used care must be taken to ensure that the body of the report is complete and that important items are not buried within an appendix from which they are unlikely ever to surface. The data contained in an appendix will be looked at by exception and in constructing appendices the researcher has made a decision on behalf of the reader that this is material which does not need to be examined in detail.

Use of colour

Colour in charts and text can make a considerable enhancement to the appearance and acceptability of a report, provided it is used wisely. Colour can be used to emphasise points, add interest and give a report a more professional appearance. The Hewlett-Packard guide to the use of colour in reports provides the following guidelines:

- use colour to **enhance** and not to decorate
- use colour to **establish patterns** and set **expectations**
- use carefully chosen colours to group similar items or concepts and to establish **correlations**
- use colour to **differentiate**
- limit the use of colour to **maximise its impact**.

The availability of low-cost ink-jet and laser colour printers and colour photocopiers means that it is possible to produce colour reports with no more difficulty than monochrome reports. To do so effectively requires that those responsible for designing the report need to have a good eye for colour. Excessive and tasteless use of colour resulting in garish reports will detract from a report rather than enhance it.

16.3 **Report Content**

A competent market research report needs to communicate what the research has found, how it found it and any limitations on the data that is presented. Beyond these general observations there is no single set of report contents that is suitable for all situations. Content will be driven by the objectives and structure of each individual survey. Nevertheless there is some common ground in terms of what a research user would expect to see as a minimum in all reports (Box 16.1).

Box 16.1 Content of a report

- **Terms of reference** – a re-statement of the reasons why the research was commissioned and the specific objectives of the research.
- **Methodology** – the research methods that were used, including the number and type of interviews, the types of respondents and any changes that were made from the original specification. The methodology may also state any limitations that should be placed on the research data – say, in terms of their significance or accuracy.
- **Summary of conclusions** – a point-by-point summary of the key findings.
- **Interpretation** – the implications of the research findings for the research user. In some cases, this may be extended to include recommendations on the marketing actions which should be considered in the light of the research findings.
- **Research findings** – tabulations and qualitative information organised by the subjects to be covered in the research.
- **Appendices** – supporting material included for reference purposes only.

The research findings will represent the main part of the report and their organisation will depend on the research objectives. They may be divided into qualitative and quantitative findings, but the topics should replicate the information objectives set out in the research proposal. The typical flow of an industrial market research report which sets out to provide a complete analysis of the market situation would be as follows:

- Market size
- Market structure
- Trends in demand
- Trends in market structure
- Spontaneous and prompted awareness of suppliers
- Analysis of customer expectations from suppliers
- Customer satisfaction with suppliers
- Purchasing procedures and supplier selection routines
- Sources of Information on suppliers
- Analysis of the activities of competitors

A competitive intelligence report which examines activities in detail could be expected to cover:

- Ownership
- Office and factory locations
- Structure of the workforce
- Management structure

- Profiles of key managers
- Production technologies
- Output by product type
- Distribution methods
- Customer base
- Key partner organisations (distributors, licences, customers)
- Financial performance
- Analysis of strengths and weaknesses
- Strategic directions.

16.4 Oral Presentations

As the saying goes 'it ain't over until the fat lady sings'. Most research programmes end with an oral presentation of findings, following which the users of the research can ask questions. The final presentation commonly takes place after the report of findings has been delivered to the client and the users of the research have has a chance to read the contents. Nevertheless, the oral presentation should contain an outline of the findings both to provide the researchers' own interpretation of what they have achieved and to set the scene for questions.

Importance of presentations

Presentations are an opportunity to add colour to what might otherwise have been a rather dry experience (Box 16.2). Whereas written reports need to be formal and to follow established conventions, oral presentations can step outside the box and use elements of showmanship to get points across, particularly when they are made to large audiences.

Box 16.2 A good presentation

The elements of a good presentation can be summarised as follows:

- Structure the material carefully in advance
- Know the material
- Use notes but do not read them
- Use high-quality visual aids
- (If possible) split the presentation task between those involved in the survey
- Respond to questions as and when the audience prefer to ask them
- Treat humour with caution
- Pace the presentation to suit the time available
- End on a high note.

Good presenters, like good report writers, are more likely to be born than trained and some researchers are congenitally incapable of performing well in front of an audience of any size. Poor presenters are best kept away from the task. Wooden, unenlightening and uninspiring presentations not only bore audiences, they can also undermine confidence in survey findings. By the same token slick presentations may prove highly entertaining and popular but if they lack substance they will prove unsatisfying when the attendees reflect back on the experience.

Structure of presentations

Presentations need to be planned carefully in advance. If they are not they risk degenerating into a series of random observations with no coherent structure. The planned structure should be communicated to the audience at the commencement of the presentation so that they know what to expect and are also in a position to indicate any items that they require the presenter to pay particular attention to. Identifying the ground the presentation is going to cover complies with the **three-part rule about making presentations**:

- tell them **what you are going to say**
- **say it**
- tell them **what you have just said**.

The introduction should also include a clear statement of what the presentation is designed to achieve. It is essential for the audience to know whether the presenter is providing a recap of the report which will act as an introduction to questions and answers or whether it is meant to be a full exposé of the findings for the benefit of an audience that has not read the report. Even if the report has been submitted in advance it is well worth remembering that a significant proportion of the audience may not have had the chance to read it.

When launching into the main body of the presentation, the presenter should know the material sufficiently well to be able to depart from the script and add colour by referring to detail – such as what particular respondents said. Notes help speakers cover the ground fully but should never be treated as a script. Unless it is delivered by an exceptionally talented presenter a script will invariably come over as wooden and boring. It also exposes the presenter to the risk of groping for responses when the script is interrupted.

Visual aids

Visual aids are essential in research presentations. Research results are normally too complex to be presented effectively without visual illustrations

---

Box 16.3 Visual aids

Designing the visual aids is an even more skilled task than drafting a report. In a research presentation, the purpose of the visual aids can be all or any of the following:

- To show research results which the presenter will explain
- To amplify or illustrate what the presenter is saying (such as quotes by respondents)
- To orientate the audience by providing a checklist of the points being covered in the presentation.

(Box 16.3). More importantly, audiences like them. Look at the faces of audiences listening to a presentation in which visual aids are being used; they are invariably watching the screen, however slight the material being projected onto it.

Recent technology has made the task of presenting visual aids substantially easier than the days when the time-consuming production of colour 35mm, overhead projector slides or posters were the only method of making an impact.

Overhead and 35 mm projectors are still widely used for presentations but major new developments in the form of electronic multimedia projection systems are gradually taking over. The main devices that are changing the face of presentations are:

- LCD panels (now themselves on their way out)
- LCD projectors
- CRT projectors
- three-dimensional cameras (the electronic equivalent of the epidiascope).

Panels and projectors linked to laptop computers enable presenters to create and show highly professional, large-screen colour presentations using features which would have been prohibitively expensive less than five years ago. The main attractions of presentation software packages such as Powerpoint, Freelance and Harvard Graphics are not only their sophistication but also their user-friendliness and the speed at which presentations can be created and adjusted. The projectors can also be linked to video recorders so that recordings of research events, such as focus groups, can be shown. Hard copy material and objects can be shown by linking projectors to three-dimensional cameras.

The methods used to show visual aids must take account of the size of the audience. Presentations to one or two individuals rarely require the use of electronic projectors to get points across and are best served by printed handouts. As audiences grow in size small-scale displays become increasingly inappropriate and technology comes into its own.

Team presentations and questions

Presentations given by a single individual can be highly successful but if a team of researchers are involved in a project it is often a good idea to let them speak for their own part of the research. This not only provides variety, it can also add depth and permits fuller responses to questions.

The ability to ask questions from the research team is one of the main reasons for presentations. It is common for presenters to state up front how they wish to handle questions. While it is very much a matter of personal preference whether questions are taken as the presentation proceeds or whether they are saved until the end, audiences will generally make the own decisions. It takes a strong presenter to hold back an audience which is determined to interpret the presentation in order to ask question as they go and the benefits of immediacy may well outweigh the dangers of the presentation overrunning or the questions anticipating points which are scheduled to come up later on.

Light relief

Far to many presenters give in to the temptation to use jokes in their presentation. A platform and a captive audience convinces many that they can try their hand at being a stand-up comedian or, even worse, they feel that it is obligatory to commence presentations with a joke. If it works, it may be fine but the risks of it not working are substantial. A good comedian is always a good presenter but not all good presenters are good comedians. Market researchers are not normally known for their comic ability and joke-telling is best left for the professionals. Apart from the problems of delivery, audiences at market research presentations are not expecting to be treated to a joke-telling session and may well regard it as an insult to their intelligence and unprofessional. Having said that, and admitting that market research is serious stuff, there is no need to invest presentations with too much gravitas. Gentle use of humour such as outrageous quotes by respondents or strange experiences during the conduct of the survey can bring light relief, help the flow of the presentation and make the points more memorable.

Pacing the presentation

Pacing the presentation to suit the time available is a rare but essential skill. Worried that they might run out of material, many researchers prepare too much which they then fail to complete or rush through in the final stages. It is difficult to assess in advance the effect the audience will have on the pace of the presentation – holding it back by asking too many questions or speeding it up by asking too few – but trial runs can be used to get the volume of material right and changes of pace during the presentation can ensure that it is completed within the allotted time.

Conclusion

Finally, far too many research presentations die out rather than come to a conclusion. There is nothing more guaranteed to let an audience down that a speaker who simply dries up when he has nothing more to say. Presentations must be brought deliberately to a conclusion, normally by a recapitulation of the most important and memorable points or a summary of conclusions, so that the audience is in no doubt that the end has been reached.

16.5 Whose Report is it Anyway?

One thing that must be clear, both in report writing and presentations, is that the conclusions drawn from a research programme must be those reached by the researchers based on the data they have obtained. Surveys are commissioned for many reasons and the results do not always accord with the preconceived ideas of the client or necessarily make the case that the client wished to have made. What use clients make of the findings in these situations is very much up to them, but researchers must resist suggestions that they modify their conclusions in order to suit some preconceived purpose for which the data was originally requested.

17 The Research Brief

Buying research involves three key stages – **briefing**, which sets out what is required by the client organisation; the **selection** of suitable organisations to carry out the research; and **obtaining a proposal**, which is the researcher's response to the briefing he has been given. This chapter describes the briefing process and Chapters 18 and 19 cover the selection of research organisations and proposals.

A survey is only as good as the initial brief. If research users fail to set out what they require it is unlikely that the right results will be obtained. A good briefing, which may comprise a briefing document and a briefing meeting, flows naturally from the initial planning process (described in Chapter 4) which resulted in the need for a survey being identified and a definition of the types of information which should be collected.

17.1 The Briefing Document

A research brief needs to contain all of the information required to assist those responsible for designing the survey (Box 17.1).

Box 17.1 The briefing document

The content of the brief should include:

- Background information
- Product or service to be researched
- Objectives of the research
- Specific information objectives
- Expectations from the research team
- Relevant internally available information on the market
- Documents
- Thoughts on the research approach
- Confidentiality
- Timing
- Budgetary constraints
- Requirements from the research companies submitting proposals
- Date by which a proposal is expected
- Contacts within the client organisation.

Background information

Background information should be given on any aspect of the company and its activities that could be relevant to the research plus the market situation in which the company operates. The need for background information will be greatest in the case of relatively unknown companies and highly specialised markets which researchers are unlikely to have encountered before. Useful background information could include:

- an **outline history** of the company
- the **nature of the market** in which it operates
- the company's **development** within the market
- **competitive organisations**
- the situation which has created the **need for research**.

The product or service to be researched

The products or services to be covered by the research should be described in full. The description should cover:

- product or service characteristics
- applications
- product or service strengths
- target markets
- price positioning
- differentiators from competitive products.

The need for a detailed description is more important in the case of technical or specialised products or services, but even in the case of well known consumer items it may be helpful to describe the attributes of the product which have helped it gain its current market share – or, in the case of a new product, the role which the product is designed to fill and why the company believes that it has a chance of succeeding.

Objectives of the research

The objectives of the research must be clearly stated in terms which are as specific as possible. They should commence with a definiton of the problem that has given rise to the need for research (such as, loss of market share, poor profit performance, difficulty in gaining access to distributors, increasing rate of customer attrition, support for new product development). The objectives should the state how information is expected to help solve the problem (such as, provide the basis for a new marketing and communication strategy or assist in the definition of the features and benefits of a new product).

Specific information objectives

The research user should identify the types of information which it is thought will meet the overall research objectives. At this stage, the list can be as comprehensive as possible, though experienced research users and others who have a feel for the magnitude of the research task should ensure that the shopping list is broadly consistent with the time and budget constraints that they subsequently identify.

Relevant information on the market

The brief can usefully contain any market data which is already available to the research user, which is thought to be accurate and which will help direct the research. Research users are sometimes reluctant to do this on the grounds that the data may be played back to them, but there is little point in paying again for information which already exists, and anything which improves the efficiency of the research process should be regarded as beneficial.

Documents

The brief should include any documention which is relevant. This would normally consist of brochures and catalogues, but it can be extended to internal reports and other evidence that might be helpful in orientating the researchers preparing the proposal.

Thoughts on the research approach

A high proportion of research users cannot make decisions on the research approach that should be adopted, are nor are they expected to. It is up to the research professionals to convince users of the best, the most cost-efficient or the least-cost routes to obtaining the data. Nevertheless, there are areas on which research users can comment and, in doing so, provide the researchers with a better idea of their requirements. Subjects which users should give some thought to include:

- **Potential sources of information** – these could include published sources, known experts on the market, technical research institutes and categories of respondent that researchers might not think of themselves
- **Opportunities to reach sources** – such as forthcoming conferences, exhibitions or trade shows.
- **Related research** already completed and potentially available.

Confidentiality

It is normal for surveys to be carried out on confidential basis and for the reults to remain the confidential property of the research sponsor. However, there are situations in which revealing the name of the client sponsoring the research is possible or even inevitable. The limits on the freedom to use the clients' name (which will normally make it easier to gain cooperation from respondents) and the requirement for confidentiality should be clearly stated in the brief. In the case of highly sensitive surveys it is increasingly common to require researchers to sign a **confidentiality agreement** before sending them the briefing document.

Timing

The brief should state clearly when the results of the research are required and, if practical, the budgetary limit that should not be exceeded. Timing is always important to research users and the delivery of the results of a research exercise will often need to be tied in with other activities that are taking place. It is helpful for the researcher to know the overall time scale that is envisioned, such as

- the dates by which the research is expected to be **commissioned**
- **key meetings** during the survey (for intermin data)
- **completion date**
- anticipated date for the final oral **presentation** of the survey findings.

Even in the best-run companies these dates may slip for reasons which are nothing to do with the research, but knowing what is expected will enable the researcher to design an approach which will meet initial plans. The only word of warning is that tight sets of commissioning and delivery deadlines which are consistently missed soon earn the company a reputation for not being serious.

Budgetary constraints

There are two diametrically opposed schools of thought on providing indications of budget available for the project in the briefing document. The first believes that researchers should be handed a problem, and it is up to them to design and cost the most appropriate research approach. The second thinks that the provision of an indication of the budget that is available will ensure that the approaches proposed are within the limits that the company can afford for the data requested.

If money is no object the first of these two alternatives poses no serious problems. Nor is it a problem if the research user already has a reasonable idea from previous experience of what the research should cost. The problem arises with naive research users who have no idea of what research can cost. For them an open-ended request for proposals will commonly result in surprises, usually unpleasant. Giving a budget indication avoids this problem, provided the budget is realistic. To get to this point the first-time research user may need to do a little preparatory research on costs part of which should be discussions with the research companies selected to submit proposals (see below).

Requirements from the research companies submitting proposals

The brief should state any information which the client particularly requires the research company to include in the proposal. This could include:

- an indication of the **feasibility** of achieving the research objectives
- an outline of **previous experience** in similar types of surveys or on similar products
- a **biographical note** on the researchers who would carry out the survey
- organisations from which the client can seek **references** on the research company.

Date by which a proposal is expected

As a separate item the briefing document should state the date by which the proposal is required. Reasonable time should be permitted for proposal preparation, taking account of the fact that the researcher may require a meeting to discuss the survey before preparing a proposal (see below). Proposal writing, particularly for large, complex research exercises requiring preliminary research, can take a considerable amount of time but the norm lies between several hours and several days.

Contacts within the client organisation

Finally, the brief should state the points of contact between the client organisation and the researcher. This should include the primary point of contact, who the proposal should be sent to, and others to whom questions can be addressed.

17.2 The Briefing Meeting

The briefing document should be sent to companies that have been shortlisted as capable of carrying out the project (see Chapter 18) together with an invitation to quote. Except in the case of the smallest and most straightforward research requirements, the submission of a briefing document should be accompanied by an offer to meet with researchers to discuss the requirement in more depth. The meeting can take place at either the client's premises or the research company offices. The former permits the client to invite additional staff members to discuss the requirement, to demonstrate products and to call for additional documentation; the latter provides an early opportunity for the client to see the research staff in their own working environment.

The purpose of the briefing meeting is to provide an opportunity for the research staff to ask questions and to get the research user to elaborate on the brief (Box 17.2). It also enables the researcher to obtain a feel for the scale of the research exercise that is expected, to obtain feedback on the likely acceptability of alternative approaches and to impress the client with his or her knowledge and competance. Both client and researcher should benefit from the exchange, the former by a better understanding of what is required and the latter through a deeper appreciation of what it is possible to obtain for the budget that is likely to be available.

Box 17.2 The briefing meeting

A briefing meeting is an opportunity to observe agency personnel in action. The indicators of agency suitability that can be gained from the meeting are:

- The **quality of the agency representative** – he or she will tend to be one of their best staff and may not be typical of the rest of the team but if s/he is not good enough the remainder are unlikely to be better.
- The level of **market and industry knowledge** that is displayed.
- The **apparent level of research skills and the ability to explain the research process**, the factors which determine the quality of the output and the compromises which may need to be made to achieve a result which is cost-effective for the client.
- The extent to which the agency is **prepared to be flexible** to meet client requirements.
- The **commercial approach of the agency** – an overtly 'hard-nosed' commercial approach may indicate that the information will be superficial; an uncommercial, academic approach may indicate that the results will be too theoretical and unusable.

---

18 Identifying Suitable Research Resources

This chapter is aimed primarily at the first-time research buyer. Companies or individuals that have already used research agencies will be tempted to stay with those that they have already seen in action and have found to be adequate. The advantages of this approach in terms of the reduction in risk are significant and even though there are occasions when fresh blood, new thinking and different skills are required, research users are generally loyal to suppliers that have served them well.

In contrast to the formality of research techniques, research buying is done more by 'gut feel' than through the application of any rigorous discipline. The adoption of ISO 9000 certification by some research companies can influence buyers to use them, particularly public sector buyers, but this is the exception rather than the rule. This chapter sets out some key decisions which research buyers need to take and provides guidelines to use when outsourcing market research from research consultancies.

18.1 In-House Resources or External Agencies

Once the information needs have been set out in the briefing document, potential **sources of research services** should be identified. Over the last decade there has been a continual trend amongst research users to outsource their research requirements from professional agencies rather than undertake studies themselves (Box 18.1). In-house research departments, once common but now rare outside the larger manufacturers of consumer products, offer a number of advantages of which the most obvious are that they develop a high level of expertise in the business in which the company is operating, became highly familiar with information sources, can network with contacts in similar businesses and can continuously track developments in markets. They can therefore obtain information efficiently and quickly. Their disadvantages are that they are unlikely to employ all of the specialist research and analysis skills that are becoming increasingly common and there is a danger that they are used only because they are there, rather than because their services are genuinely required.[1] The compromise solution for those organisations that do not require a complete research facility but do not wish to dispense completely with an in-house research resource is to employ a marketing services market research or business intelligence manager whose role is to act as the **interface between internal users of**

Box 18.1 Outsourcing

Outsourcing offers a number of advantages which in-house services find it difficult to replicate. The most important of these are:

- Anonymity
- Objectivity
- Cross-fertilisation

- Specialist resources
- Intermittent services
- Cost-savings.

---

research and external suppliers of research services. The internal manager specifies the research requirement in conjunction with the research user, buys services from an external research company and interprets the research findings using his or her internal knowledge.

Anonymity

For many research exercises, particularly in new-product research or competitor analysis, it is imperative that the survey is not associated with the sponsor; this is difficult to achieve if the research is carried out by the sponsor themself. Independent research agencies can guarantee anonymity, though in order to do so they may make the task of getting information from respondents more difficult. It is increasingly common, especially in industrial research for respondents to ask for the identity of the research sponsor, and if this cannot be given they may decline to be interviewed.

Objectivity

All research data needs to be objective and unbiased if it is to be useful. It also needs to be **seen to be** unbiased. Internal research resources risk being exposed to the cross-currents of opinion within the sponsoring organisation and may inadvertently permit them to colour their findings. More importantly, an external agency can be isolated from the internal debate and the results they present can be shown to be free of any bias.

Anonymity is a method of increasing the objectivity of the information given by respondents. Knowledge of who the information is for may well encourage biased responses. The best method of ensuring cooperation and maintaining objectivity is to reveal the name of the research sponsor only at the end of the interview. This sometimes produces a bonus in the form of additional comments about the client organisation.

Cross-fertilisation

Internal researchers develop valuable expertise in their industry sector, which may improve the efficiency of the research process and the depth of analysis. However, an external agency generally sees many different market sectors and is in a position to import new thinking and fresh solutions.

Specialist resources

Because they meet the needs of a broad range of clients, external agencies can invest in hardware and develop specialist data collection and analytical skills which are beyond the resources of an internal research unit.

Intermittent services

An external agency is employed only when its services are required. The continuous availability of internal research staff may lead to the generation of low-priority problems just to keep them busy.

Cost savings

By not imposing a continuous overhead burden on the company the use of external agencies tends to result in lower costs than the maintenance of an internal department.

18.2 Identifying Potential External Suppliers

The steps in identifying potential research companies are reasonably straightforward.

Classified lists

The first is to obtain a classified list of market research companies which identifies their:

- research specialisations
- types of data and/or research services offered
- skills in specific products or industry sectors
- size (personnel and sales)
- countries they cover
- some of the clients they have serviced.

The most common sources of lists are the market research trade or professional organisations active in each country, and international listings. The key sources are the *Organisations' Book*, published by the Market Research Society, the American Marketing Association list of research companies, the ESOMAR membership list and lists made available by specialist industry groups such as the European Chemical Market Research Association and the Society of Competitive Intelligence Professionals

(SCIP). Some associations, such as the British Market Research Association (BMRA), offer **computerised matching services** which put research users in touch with suppliers offering the specific skills or experience they require. Marketing magazines and buyers' guides for marketing services also contain lists of market research companies, but they are rarely complete. The internet hosts a number of web sites which list market research companies, and there are also the web sites of the research companies themselves. Company listings on the internet need to be treated with some caution since they often contain only those organisations that have registered with the site operator. This is not to say that the companies listed are unsuitable, only that the lists are incomplete. Published listings are still better, to the extent that they apply some criteria before an organisation can be included. For inclusion in the *Market Research Society Organisations' Book*, companies must employ a full member of the society and agree to abide by the society's Code of Practice.

Syndicated research reports

The second step is to obtain a list of syndicated research reports and their publishers – Marketsearch, Findex and Predicasts list market surveys and data that can be purchased off the shelf. Data available off the shelf may provide a solution to the problem and many report publishers will also carry out ad hoc projects using the data they have already collected as a starting point. If this route is chosen, be sure to check that the data they collect for a single client is not subsequently used in their published reports.

Known users

Finally, ask known users of research, trade associations and business consultants (including the Business Links) for qualified suggestions on suitable research agencies. This an excellent method, in that anyone recommending a research company should also be in a position to identify their strengths and weaknesses. It falls down only to the extent that research users and consultants tend to have only limited experience with research companies and may miss out one that is ideally suited to a particular task.

18.3 Assessing the Suitability of Suppliers

Whenever a research company is offering data for sale, either in the form of a published report, a multi-client survey or panel survey results, the purchasing process is simplified because the buyer can have some advance sight of what s/he is buying. S/he can also satisfy themself that the methodology was appropriate and can ask other users whether they regard the results as being accurate. In the case of ad hoc surveys, which are custom designed to suit a client's specific requirements there is a problem in that there is only minimal tangible evidence to indicate the agency's ability to obtain the information required. Nevertheless, there are other indicators of apparent suitability, namely:

- Size and organisational structure
- Personnel
- Field resources
- Supervision and control
- Apparent compatibility with the client organisation
- Track record
- References
- Premises
- Responsiveness
- Brochures and internet sites
- Previous reports.

Size and organisational structure

Research is a business for which the cost of entry is low. This results in a proliferation of sole traders and small companies working alongside medium-sized and large companies. The size and legal format of the organisation says little about their suitability to carry out any individual project, but it is essential to recognise that not all organisations will have the skills and resources to carry out projects equally well. A small specialist unit may be ideal if they have directly relevant experience and/or the top person is going to devote a high proportion of their time to the project. Even so, large complex surveys may be better carried out by companies with substantial resources, a broad range of skills and a management and supervisory structure.

There is a perennial question about whether it is better to be a 'big fish in a little pond or a little fish in a big pond'. The advantage of being a major client to an agency is that it will normally result in preferential treatment. No agency wants to lose its major source of business and will tend to perform consistently well to ensure that this does not happen. The size of company in which this can be achieved depends entirely on the volume of business that is to be placed.

Personnel

The quality of all projects is dependent on the research managers and the research executives that will carry them out. The educational background and research experience of staff is a primary indicator of suitability. Particular attention should be paid to the senior staff assigned to the account since it is their abilities, even more than those of the research executives, that will determine the quality of the research. Beware of the professional salesperson who has a high order of skill but will vanish off the scene as soon as a contract is placed. S/he has a role to play but may not have the time or the ability to influence the quality of the project.

Field resources

The quality of the data collection process is equally heavily dependent on the quality of the field interviewers. For large-scale surveys, the size of the fieldforce, its geographical distribution, its organisation, the experience and skills of the field interviewers, the number of CATI stations and the quality of field supervision are key issues to be examined. If fieldwork is to be subcontracted to a third party field agency, commonly the case for smaller research companies and whenever researchers are working outside the limits of their own resources (e.g. overseas), the skills and resources of the specialist need to be examined.

Supervision and control

The level of involvement of the management of the agency in the conduct of the survey is an important indicator of quality. Most clients will be best serviced by an organisation which involves its senior and most experienced staff in the specification of the research, monitoring progress and the interpretation of the findings. Indications of excessive delegation to junior staff should be treated as a serious warning signal.

Apparent compatibility

The research process requires considerable interaction between the client and the agency. The primary contact in the agency therefore needs to be a person who not only has the appropriate level of skill but also commands the confidence and respect of the client as well as being sensitive to the client's requirements.

Track record

Relevant experience can be an important indicator since it is likely to shorten the learning curve within the agency and will enable them to bring a higher level of industry knowledge to the problem. However, it is important to distinguish between the experience of the company and that of the individuals within it. Company experience may be irrelevant if the individuals that gained it have left. Individual experience is relevant regardless of the company within which it was gained.

References

A list of previous clients that the company has serviced says something about the quality and character of the business, but does not indicate whether the clients were satisfied with what they were provided. It can be useful to obtain references from previous clients – but remember that agencies will refer potential clients only to their successes, not their failures.

Premises

A visit to the agency's premises will show whether the physical resources of the company appear to match their written or oral statements. A visit permits observation of the approximate number of staff, the type of staff employed, the corporate culture and the quality and organisation of the premises. Lavish premises can be variously interpreted. They may indicate that the organisation is successful, believes that a good working environment is conducive to quality workmanship and that it looks after its staff. It may also suggest that the fees are high. Poor-quality premises may suggest that the fees will be low but also that the quality of the research output will also be low. Most high-quality research companies fall between these two extremes.

Responsiveness

A company will be at its best when in the process of winning business; any shortfalls in responsiveness at this stage could indicate that there will be more serious delays once surveys are actually commissioned.

Brochures and internet sites

Sales literature has to be treated with caution but its quality and content says something about the company. Poor brochure material is probably more significant than high-quality documentation. It is relatively easy to put a good brochure together and a company that is not concerned with brochure quality may not be committed to the overall quality of its service.

Internet sites are also easy to construct but a number of companies use them as an opportunity to demonstrate their expertise. A simple, well designed and interesting site can be equally as effective as a good brochure but the internet provides an opportunity to extend data provision to include texts on research techniques, examples of surveys, staff profiles, references from satisfied clients and other material which can boost confidence in the company's abilities.

Previous reports

Beware of the agency that offers to show you custom reports completed for previous clients – they may be equally cavalier with your survey results. It is sometimes possible for an agency to show reports, such as when the client has given permission to do so or when the client is no longer active in the business, but a reputable agency will make this plain before sight of any documents is offered.

18.4 Compiling a Short-list

The review of research agencies should be used to compile a short-list of potential suppliers who are apparently capable of carrying out the survey satisfactorily. The short-list should contain a maximum of three or four agencies – any more will impose a heavy burden when briefing potential suppliers, will tend to be confusing during the evaluation of proposals and is unfair on the research business, given the effort required from them in the next stages of the selection process. Furthermore, research agencies will tend to put far more effort into the preparation of their proposals if they have a one in three or four chances of success, rather than a lottery involving tens of suppliers.

The shortlist will tend to gravitate towards companies that appear to have the right background, but it is advantageous to select companies of different sizes and types since they will be likely to construct different approaches. There are often a range of alternative approaches which can be adopted to collecting data and it is useful to consider them before finally deciding.

18.5 Approved Research Contractors

In Chapter 17 it was suggested that a meeting with research agencies should take place after a brief has been issued. It can also be advantageous to seek a meeting **before** a brief is issued, or even at a stage when no specific research project is in mind. Companies intending to use research regularly should have a short-list of agencies they could use and which covers all of the skills and resources they are likely to require. Some companies which contain a number of divisions that could commission research projects go as far as having an approved list of suppliers from which all vendors have to be chosen. Vetting suitable research companies is a time-consuming process which should be repeated as infrequently as possible. Educating research companies into the practices, ways of thinking and the specific requirements of an individual client is also a lengthy process which is best carried out with a limited number of potential suppliers and will pay major dividends in getting what is required.

Note

1. For a good discussion of the advantages and disadvantages of internal services see Aubrey Wilson 'The Internal Service Department – Justifying Your Existence', *Logistics Information Management*, 11(1) (MCB University Press, 1998).

19 Selecting Research Consultants

The final stage in commissioning a research project is the selection of the research contractor to use. Buying research is much like buying any other intangible service and has a lot in common with selecting lawyers, accountants and management consultants. The objective is to select an organisation that is comfortable to work with and will deliver competent research at a price that matches the budget available.

19.1 The Proposal

Those invited to quote should respond with a proposal which will be the basis for selection of the research agency to be used. At its simplest in situations where the client has provided a very precise specification of what is required (number of interviews, interview type, interview length, sample methodology and analysis routines) the proposal will contain the agencies credentials, a response to any questions raised in the brief, suggestions for improving the project or reducing costs and a fee. Where the brief does little more than outline the problem the proposal needs to be much fuller (Box 19.1).

It should be borne in mind that some agencies write better proposals than research documents, but the content, format, presentation and amount of thought provided in the proposal should give a reasonable guide to the ability of the agency.

Box 19.1 The proposal

- **Objectives** of the research
- **Information** to be sought
- **Research approach**, types of research techniques to be deployed and numbers of interviews, group discussions, etc.
- **Methods** by which the results will be presented to the client, including the structure of the written report and the number and format of meetings
- **Cost**
- **Time** the survey will take to complete
- **Research team** and their qualifications
- Any **related experience** the agency has.

When evaluating proposals there are a number of indications of the suitability and competence of the agencies that have prepared them. The most important is the amount of thought that has gone into the **definition of the information to be sought and the research methodology**. Proposals which merely add a cost figure to the brief suggest that the agency has not given much thought to what is required, and may not fully understand the problem. High levels of **value-added** in the form of analysing the research objectives, adding questions which will enhance the ability of the project to solve the specified problem and creative thought to the methods of obtaining the information are all signs of an organisation that is not only competent but is genuinely interested in carrying out the project. Marks should also be given for a proposal which suggests alternative approaches which result in different costs – thus permitting the client to match the research with the budget that is available.

19.2 Paid-for Proposals

One method to ensure that quality proposals are obtained is to offer to pay for them – in other words treat the proposal as a consultancy exercise in its own right. The time commitment to proposal writing can be considerable and while the desire to win the project will normally ensure that agencies commit the resources willingly, they will tend to be far more creative if paid.

19.3 Assessing Alternative Offers

There are nine primary yardsticks by which the quality and suitability of alternative offers should be assessed (Box 19.2).

Cost will be a primary consideration for most research buyers and one aspect of proposals which sometimes surprises clients is the extreme variations in the cost quotations they receive. The cost of a research project is normally made up of a daily rate for executive time, the fees paid for interviews, overheads and expenses. In most countries when comparing like for like the costs tend to be very similar (Box 19.3 on page 200).

While the above can all be true, the most likely reason for variation in the cost of proposals produced in response to an identical brief is that the different agencies have interpreted the brief differently and are **offering different solutions**. This may not be obvious from the words contained in the proposal and before accepting a low-cost proposal, or dismissing one which is offered at a high cost, it is well worth discussing the offers in detail in order to understand precisely what the differences are due to.

Box 19.2 Assessing alternative offers

- The degree to which the research vendor **understands** the marketing situation of the research user and the purposes for which the research is required.
- The extent to which the offer meets the **information requirements** specified in the brief.
- The extent to which the proposal shows that the agency has thought about the problem and has modified the approach and the information yield to provide a **better overall result** for the client.
- The proposed **methodology** for collecting information and the likely success in achieving the information objectives.
- The extent to which the methodology is **caveated** – vague promises and caveats may be used as a justification why important items of information are omitted from the report that is finally delivered.
- **Presentation** – be wary of proposals which are double spaced and printed on thick paper to give an impression of bulk.
- **Irrelevant content** – be equally wary of proposals which contain a high proportion of standard and irrelevant content which is obviously designed to impress, is included in all proposals but does nothing to help the reader assess the suitability of the agency.
- **Language** – the use of research jargon which is well above the head of the non-research trained reader is a sign that the researchers may be too academic to relate to the research users.
- **Cost**.

Research data which is sold on a syndicated basis should automatically represent good value for money because the research costs are shared. In the case of very large-scale surveys, syndication may be essential since no individual client will be prepared to put up the entire research cost on their own. The subscription each client is charged is a function of the number of sales the research company thinks they will make, as well as the total cost incurred. Low subscriptions tend to result in the data reaching a wide audience, whereas high subscriptions ensure a certain amount of exclusivity.

19.4 **Presentation of Proposals**

In the case of large complex assignments the research agencies may be invited to present their proposals to the client organisation. This provides the agency with an opportunity to stress the reasons why they feel they are suited to carry out the research. It provides the client with an opportunity to ask further questions and test the statements made in the proposal.

Box 19.3 Reasons for cost variations

That variations in cost can occur for a number of **fundamental reasons**, including:

- The fact that the executives employed on the project are of differing levels of seniority and are remunerated at different rates – even sole traders can operate at significantly different daily fee rates, depending on the experience that they have and their confidence that they can persuade clients that they are worth higher rates.
- The interviewers have different skill levels which effects their remuneration rates.
- The overhead structure varies in that there are greater or lesser levels of supervision and the costs of the premises differ because of quality or location.
- The relative efficiencies of the organisations differ, some working on higher numbers of interviews per day and lower inputs of executive time than others to achieve any given result.
- Varying levels of profit expectations.

Other factors which can cause significant variations in cost are:

- Differing interpretations of the difficulty of obtaining the data that is sought – this may affect the length of interview that is quoted for.
- The fact that some agencies may already posseses data which will contribute to the solution.
- The level of contact time between agency and client that has been budgeted.
- The desire, or lack of desire, to cost keenly in order to win the contract.

19.5 Negotiations

A more acceptable but higher-cost proposal does not have to be accepted without negotiation. The days when research agencies regarded themselves as professionals who did not discuss fees are long over and there is always a deal to be done. Normally this will involve a compromise between trimming the methodology – trimming the information yield and cutting the agency's profit margin.

20 Controlling the Research Process

Good research projects result from a effective working relationship between clients and research agencies. Each partner in the relationship must contribute the knowledge and skill that they derive from their respective background in order to get the most from the research budget. Although it may be tempting to clients to let the research agency implement the project without interaction (or interfering), this can result in the results being less satisfactory.

Clients require skills to manage their relationships with outside agencies so that they can make an effective contribution to the research process. This is most applicable to ad hoc research. Where data is being purchased off the shelf, less interaction with the research agency is needed and the findings can be viewed in advance to ensure that they are what is required; but even then, if special analysis of the data is required, the research process needs to be managed by the client.

The steps by which clients can make an effective contribution to projects are:

- a full briefing of the research team prior to the commencement of the research
- questionnaire approval
- regular progress reports during the survey
- regular reviews of the information yield
- an independent assessment of the quality of the results.

20.1 Project Briefing or 'Kick-Off' Meeting

At the commencement of all research projects representatives of the client should meet the entire research team and brief them personally to ensure that they are equipped with all the information they need to carry out the survey efficiently and within the time deadlines set for the research. To some extent this overlaps with the briefing for the proposal, but this time it is aimed at the researchers themselves rather than the agency's managers. The topics that a typical project team briefing should cover are:

- company, background and project ranges
- reasons for commissioning the research
- decisions that the research is intended to support

- key characteristics of the market to be studied
- market information that is relevant and non-confidential
- characteristics of respondents
- lists or sources of lists of respondents
- client actions
- timetable.

Company, background and product ranges

If the client is using a research agency for the first time the briefing should cover the company, its structure and its product ranges. This should include passing over any brochures and technical literature which describe the products that are to be covered by the research.

Reasons for commissioning the research

The reasons for commissioning the research should be covered in depth. This will provide the researchers with a clear idea of why they are being employed and will increase their sensitivity to information which may not be in the original brief but which may prove to be available and relevant to the problem that the company is facing.

Decisions that the research is intended to support

The key decisions which the company is facing should be described, together with the relevance of the data to those decisions. This will be particularly relevant during the interpretation of the research findings.

Key characteristics of the market to be studied (where known)

Researchers need to be as fully briefed as possible on the structure of the market and its characteristics. This will help them organise the research and ensure that all relevant segments and sources of information are covered.

Market information that is relevant and non-confidential

There is no point in asking research staff to re-generate what is already in existence and any data which will assist the researchers to set up the research programme, design the questionnaire, carry out their analysis and verify their findings should be provided.

The characteristics of respondents

If anything is known about the characteristics of respondents, these should be discussed. The identification and qualification of respondents in terms of their suitability to provide information are key issues, particularly when covering specialist products which have a low market penetration.

Lists or sources of lists of respondents

Where clients hold their own or independently sourced lists of respondents which are to be used in the research, these should be passed over or arrangements made to make them available to the research staff.

Client actions

Any actions to be taken by the client, such as the provision of samples or the preparation of display materials, need to be agreed, together with the timing of their availability.

Timetable

The timetable for the research programme should be agreed, together with milestone events, reporting points and meetings.

20.2 **Review of Questionnaires**

Clients are not expected to be experts on questionnaire design, but a review of the questionnaires and checklists to be used in the resarch is usually helpful. Clients can make a valuable contribution to the questions themselves, technical terms and anticipated responses.

20.3 **Progress Reports**

Throughout the duration of the project the client should seek regular formal and informal **updates of progress**. These should be designed to ensure that the project is running on time, that the data that is required is being obtained, whether modifications to the research approach or the information yield are needed and whether there are additional contributions that the client can make to the survey. Progress meetings can take the form of informal telephone contact and interim presentations at which findings are presented and discussed.

20.4 **Revisions to Information Yield**

Once a project has commenced it is normally too late to change the research specification without incurring a cost penalty. This means that arbitrary changes should be avoided, but does not preclude changes that arise from the research process itself. These are likely to include:

- Data which is proving unobtainable
- Data covering additional aspects of the market not anticipated at the briefing or proposal writing stage but subsequently found to be important
- Incremental data which is a by-product of the chosen research methodology, and is useful
- Extensions to additional markets or market sectors not anticipated in the original research approach.

20.5 Initial Review of Results

An oral presentation of the findings once the data has been analysed but prior to a report being written can alert the client to the conclusions and permit a contribution to the interpretation of the data and the structuring of the report. This can include the specification of analysis which the research team may not have considered.

20.6 Final Review of Findings

Once the report has been written the research team has a vital contribution to play in selling the research findings to company management that will use the data. This is best achieved by permitting management to understand – and, if necessary, challenge – the methodology, research findings, interpretation and conclusions reached by the research team (see Chapter 16).

20.7 Assessing the Quality of the Results

An issue of paramount importance to all research users is the **accuracy and comprehensiveness** of the results obtained from a research programme and whether they are of sufficient quality to support the decisions that are to be taken. The comprehensiveness of the data is relatively easy to establish, but assessing accuracy requires a series of checks during and after the research programme.

There are six key indications that the survey results are accurate.

Survey implementation

Was the proposed survey methodology applied rigorously, and have any departures from plan been explained satisfactorily?

Bias

Were there any factors or events which arose during the survey which could have biased the results?

Statistical checks

Can the level of statistical accuracy of the findings be demonstrated?

Internal consistency of the results

Are the various sets of data within the survey findings consistent with each other?

Consistency with independent data

Are the findings consistent with internal data on the market or previous surveys on the subject?

Consistency with management expectations

How well do the findings fit with internal opinion on the subject, conventional wisdom or common sense?

21 Research Ethics

Ethics – or what is deemed to be good or bad in human conduct – has become a key issue in market research, just as it has in many other areas of business practice. Research is particularly prone to ethical assessment partly because there are many who regard it as an invasion of privacy, and therefore inherently unethical, and partly because research has been abused. Typical abuses include misrepresentation of research results to 'prove' a point and use of a market survey as a cover for some other information gathering or selling activity. Business and competitive intelligence are even more prone to censure on the grounds that they are unethical because the information they seek may be regarded as confidential.

Some of the practices which have resulted in a poor reputation for research are not only unethical but also illegal. Fraud, bribery, trespass, misrepresentation and illegal surveillance are all grounds for criminal proceedings, and have all been used at some stage by individuals and organisations who set no limits on how far they are prepared to go in order to acquire commercial information which cannot be obtained by legitimate and wholly ethical methods (Box 21.1).

It is widely accepted that it is perfectly ethical for information to be collected on consumers' purchases and retail sales, but does the same apply to a container manufacturer revealing how many units he ships to a specific customer or an equipment manufacturer revealing the type, size and capacity of the machinery he has sold? Unless they have signed a confidentiality agreement, the container and machinery manufacturers are acting ethically, but their customer may not agree.

Suspicion of research is impossible to dispel completely but research practitioners and those that use them need to do all they can to ensure that suspicions are not confirmed by unethical research procedures and the misuse of research data. The professional bodies for market research and competitive intelligence have developed codes of practice which they require all members to adhere to in order to retain their membership. These define the basis on which ethical research must be carried out and are generally adhered to by legitimate research practitioners.

21.1 Key Ethical Issues

The key ethical issues which relate to research can be grouped under three headings, which relate to:

- respondents
- research agencies and research staff
- research users.

Box 21.1 Industrial espionage and market research

The boundary between industrial espionage and market research is defined very clearly by the techniques which are used. Research can only ever be carried out on a basis in which:

- written sources used are all in the public domain
- direct sources are aware of the purpose of the enquiries that are being made
- direct sources of information are free to cooperate or not.

Although industrial espionage may also use open research techniques, it can also revert to covert approaches in which:

- respondents are unaware of the true purpose of the enquiries
- information is collected without the 'owner's' knowledge
- unethical or illegal techniques are used.

The distinction seems to be very clear, but is not always acknowledged by those who prefer to categorise all information gathering techniques as a form of spying. Unfortunately there are too many grey areas which can confuse the issue. For example, where on the following list of techniques used to estimate the sales of suppliers into a market does the transition from ethical to unethical occur?

- Grossing up from purchases made by a sample of customers
- Analysis of the sales made by retail outlets
- Estimates made on the basis of ingredient purchases by manufacturers
- Estimates made on the basis of the production machinery used and its capacity
- Estimates based on purchases of packaging
- Estimates obtained in the course of discussions with the company's staff
- Estimates based on statements by staff who have left the company.

Respondents

The main issues with respondents are:

- disclosure of information relating to the purpose of the survey and the uses to which the data will be put
- maintaining respondents' freedom to participate in a research exercise or not
- establishing the bona fides of the research agency
- the protection of respondents' identity
- non-disclosure of the information provided by specific respondents
- protection from selling under the guise of research (sugging).

The **respondent is the most valuable asset** that the research business has and anything which reduces respondents' willingness to cooperate in future surveys is not only unfortunate for the respondents but will also undermine the ability of researchers to collect information. In practice, only a small proportion of the population have ever participated in research programmes but there is a much higher level of awareness of research and if awareness is accompanied by adverse opinion it can be a powerful disincentive to cooperate.

In order to permit an informed decision on whether to participate in a survey, respondents should be told the **purpose of the survey and the uses to which the data resulting from the survey will be put**. Whether the name of the sponsor of the survey is revealed or not depends on the background to the research. There are perfectly valid research and marketing reasons for withholding the identity of the research sponsor and these may need to be explained to respondents.

No form of coercion should be applied in order to induce respondents to participate in a research exercise. Although it is perfectly legitimate to offer some form of inducements such as an honorarium, a gift or an entry into a prize draw, there can be no use of excessive persuasion, intimidation or abuse. Even if respondents agree to participate in a survey they must retain the right to refuse to answer specific questions which they regard as being an **intrusion of their privacy**.

Part of the process by which respondents can establish for themselves that a research exercise is genuine lies in the establishment of the **bona fides of the research agency** that is carrying out the research. Although some research agencies are well known, even to the general public, most are not and interviewer identity cards, letters sent in advance requesting cooperation or the opportunity to call the research agency can all be used to convince respondents that they are dealing with reputable organisations.

In all research exercises it is essential that the **identities of respondents** are **protected** – unless for some reason they have given permission for their identity to be revealed. Industrial respondents commonly invite interviewers to communicate their identity to the research sponsor in order to find out more about the product or service being researched, but in most instances respondents need to be given a guarantee of anonymity which is strictly adhered to. Furthermore there must be no way that research sponsors can link specific items of information with specific respondents. The use of market research as a means of building databases of potential customers is an absolute taboo.

Under no circumstances should there be a link between market research and selling. Apart from the fact that any association between the two might distort the research findings, there must be no risk that respondents will be exposed to a sales approach as a result of having participated in a survey. The use of research as a cover for selling, one of the most common abuses of research, is an activity that the research business has long sought to eliminate. Although it is perfectly permissible for a salesman to seek information about those he is attempting to sell to, it is unethical for him to disguise himself as a market researcher in order to obtain information **prior to commencing a sales pitch**.

The front-line information collectors in all research exercises are the interviewers and the protection of respondents is to a large extent in their hands. In the case of personal interviews, the difficulties of imposing standards on part-time employees who spend very little time in the research companies' offices should not be underestimated. Telephone interviewing from central sites with supervision is much easier to control but in all cases to ensure compliance with the highest ethical standards, interviewer training must include the actions and statements they can and cannot make. Any reported infringements should be dealt with severely.

Research agencies and research staff

The key ethical issues for research agencies and their staff are:

- client confidentiality
- protection of client interests
- the reuse of data
- the basis on which research is carried out
- the quality of the research programme
- research staff assigned to the project.

Respondent anonymity, discussed above, is often matched by a need to keep the identity of the client confidential. Most research programmes become common knowledge in the industry quite quickly but in the case of new-product research or the testing of new marketing initiatives it may be detrimental to the client if their identity is disclosed. Confidentiality also applies to the disclosure of any information revealed to the research agency in order to assist them carry out the research programme. No agency would stay in business for long if they were associated with information leaks but procedures must be put in place to ensure that client data is not revealed to third parties. Discussions about the research with third parties, press releases, articles or conference presentations describing the research cannot take place **unless the client has given permission**.

It is axiomatic that the clients' interests must be protected at all times. This not only involves maintaining confidentiality but also an undertaking that a directly competitive study for a rival company cannot be carried out for a defined period of time, commonly 18 months or 2 years. Similarly, the data obtained from a field research programme cannot be recycled either in a report for another client or in a multi-client survey. Clearly this does not apply to published information, which by its nature is non-proprietary, nor to the experience of using particular research techniques or the methods of interpreting data, which are the tools of the research executives' trade. It would, however, apply to a research approach which a client has developed internally for their own use and which they train an external research agency to use on their behalf.

In carrying out a survey it is unethical for a research agency to misrepresent who they are, what they are doing and the client they are working for. It is acceptable, indeed sometimes necessary, to withhold information about a survey but researchers cannot make statements which are designed to **mislead respondents**.

Research companies and their staff must **deliver the research programme that the client has paid for**. Unless alterations in methodology and coverage are agreed in advance with the client, the number and type of interviews, the content of the questionnaire and the depth and quality of the analysis should be as set out in the research proposal. If there are deviations which cannot be agreed with the client, they must be explained and their impact on the results stated. The report that is delivered to the client must be a fair representation of what was found. Spurious levels of accuracy must not be claimed and, where relevant, the levels of significance of the data should be stated. If for any reason the research programme failed to work or did not yield the quality of results that were expected, this should be admitted and a course of corrective action agreed.

Finally, many clients like to know which research staff will be assigned to a project before they take a decision to commission. In contrast, research agencies prefer to keep their options open until the research is due to commence. The critical issue is usually who will be assigned to direct the project. Research users know that the quality of the outcome of a research programme is highly dependent on the personnel assigned to it. Agencies who fail to declare that the senior and highly convincing staff used to sell a project will have no further input to the research process are engaging in a deception which may be detrimental to the client's interests.

Research users

The main ethical considerations for research users are the calls they make on research agency time and use they make of the data. The key issues are:

- soliciting research proposals for research they never intend to commission
- the number of proposals they solicit
- asking for more than they have paid for
- misusing research data.

It is not unknown for research users to solicit research proposals for research they never intend to commission. Good proposals contain a valuable blueprint for carrying out a research programme and picking a research agencies' brains in this way is a form of theft, unless it is made plain that the offer is highly speculative. An equally unattractive practice is seeking a proposal in order to reach a minimum number of offers, when the decision on who is to carry out the research has already been taken. Research agencies can sometimes detect when they are being used as a makeweight but, if not, they are being deliberately placed in a position in which they will waste their time.

The number of proposals which clients should solicit is a constant source of debate. It is normal and perfectly acceptable to solicit three proposals. Much more than this decreases the chances of success to the point where agencies may feel that quoting is a waste of time. In cases where it is genuinely difficult to decide the type of agency that should be invited to quote it is preferable to have a **pre-tendering process**, which relies on information which agencies can provide easily, and then make a short-list of apparently suitable agencies.

When a survey is completed it is desirable and perfectly legitimate for research users to ask questions about the research process, the accuracy of the findings and about additional facts or interpretations which might be available as a by-product. It is unethical to regard the research as unsatisfactory if it cannot be stretched to cover subjects not included in the original brief or which are beyond the capacity of the research approach that has been adopted. The problem is compounded if clients use a threat of non-payment to induce agencies to carry out work beyond the original budget.

Finally, the misuse or misrepresentation of research results, either internally or externally, is unethical. This includes the suppression of unacceptable parts of the research findings, the imaginative reworking of results to achieve a desired conclusion and the use of partial data to support a false claim.

Further Reading

General market research

M. Baker, *Research for Marketing* (London: Macmillan, 1991).
R. Birn, P. Hague and P. Vangelder (eds), *A Handbook of Market Research Techniques* (London: Kogan Page, 1991).
A. Blankenship, *Professional Telephone Surveys* (New York: McGraw-Hill, 1977).
U. Bradley, *Applied Marketing and Social Research* (London: John Wiley, 1987).
P. Chisnall, *Marketing Research* (London: McGraw-Hill, 1991).
P. Hague, *The Industrial Marketing Research Handbook* (London: Kogan Page, 1990).
N. K. Malhotra, *Marketing Research: An Application Orientation* (Englewood Cliffs, NJ: Prentice-Hall, 1993).
K. McDaniel, *Marketing Research Essentials* (Cincinnati, OH: South-Western College Publishing, 1998).
K. Sutherland (ed.), *Researching Business Markets* (London: Kogan Page, 1991).
D. Tull and D. Hawkins, *Marketing Research – Measurement and Method* (New York: St Martin's Press, 1990).
A. Wilson, *The Assessment of Industrial Markets* (London: Hutchinson, 1968).
R. Worcester and J. Downham (eds), *Consumer Market Research Handbook* (The Hague: Elsevier, 1986).

Competitive intelligence

R. Duro and B. Sandstrom, *The Basic Principles of Marketing Warfare* (Chichester: John Wiley, 1987).
L. Fuld, *The New Competitive Intelligence* (New York: John Wiley, 1995).
L. Kahaner, *Competitive Intelligence: From Black Ops to Boardrooms – How to Gather, Analyse and Use Information to Succeed in the Global Marketplace* (New York: Simon & Schuster, 1996).
R. Linville, *CI Boot Camp* (Alexandria, VA: Society of Competitive Intelligence Professionals, 1996).
M. Porter, *Competitive Advantage* (New York: St Martin's Press, 1985).
M. Porter, *Competitive Strategy* (New York: The Free Press, 1980).
A. Ries and J. Trout, *Marketing Warfare* (New York: McGraw-Hill, 1986).
I. Winkler, *Corporate Espionage: What Is It, Why It's Happening In Your Company, What You Must Do About It* (Rocklin, CA: Prima Publishing, 1997).

Research applications

D. Bernstein, *Company Image and Reality* (Eastbourne: Holt, Rinehart & Winston, 1986).
A. Dutka, *AMA Handbook for Customer Satisfaction* (Lincolnwood, IL: NTC Business Books, 1993).
B. Gale, *Managing Customer Value* (New York: The Free Press, 1994).
M. Hanan and P. Karp, *Customer Satisfaction* (New York: Amacom, 1989).
R. Hill and T. Hillier, *Organisational Buying Behaviour* (London: Macmillan, 1986).
F. Webster and Y. Wind, *Organizational Buying Behaviour* (Englewood Cliffs, NJ: Prentice-Hall, 1972).

Marketing texts with research content

P. Kotler, *Marketing Management: Analysis, Planning and Control*, 5th edn (Englewood Cliffs, NJ: Prentice-Hall, 1984).
D. Mercer, *Marketing*, 2nd edn (Oxford: Blackwell, 1996).
S. Paliwoda, *International Marketing*, 2nd edn (Oxford: Butterworth-Heinemann, 1995).

Techniques useful to researchers

D. Bernstein, *Put Together, Put It Across* (London: Cassell, 1988).
B. Cooper, *Writing Technical Reports* (Harmondsworth: Penguin, 1964).
E. Gowers, *The Complete Plain Words* (London: HMSO, 1954).
R. Hoff, *'I Can See You Naked': A Fearless Guide to Making Presentations* (Kansas City, MS: Andrews & McMeel, 1988).
J. Honeycutt, *Using the Internet*, 3rd edn (Indianapolis, IN: Que, 1997).
R. Jolles, *How to Run Seminars and Workshops* (New York: John Wiley, 1993).
M. Moroney, *Facts from Figures* (Harmondsworth: Penguin, 1992).
E. Tufte, *The Visual Display of Quantitative Information* (Cheshire, CT: Graphics Press, 1983).
K. Waterhouse, *English, Our English* (London: Viking Books, 1992).

Knowledge management

V. Allee, *The Knowledge Evolution – Expanding Organisational Intelligence* (London: Butterworth-Heinemann, 1997).
T. Davenport and L. Prusak, *Working Knowledge: How Organisations Manage what They Know* (Boston: Harvard Business School Press, 1997).
R. Ruggles (ed.) *Knowledge Management Tools – Resources for the Knowledge Based Economy* (London: Butterworth–Heinemann, 1997).

Index